The Ten Rules
of Sam Walton

The Ten Rules of Sam Walton

Success Secrets for Remarkable Results

Michael Bergdahl

Foreword by Rob Walton,
Chairman of the Board, Wal-Mart Stores, Inc.

WILEY

John Wiley & Sons, Inc.

Published by John Wiley & Sons, Inc., Hoboken, New Jersey.
Published simultaneously in Canada.

For general information on our other products and services, or technical support, please contact our Customer Care Department within the United States at (800) 762-2974, outside the United States at (317) 572-3993 or fax (317) 572-4002.

Wiley also publishes its books in a variety of electronic formats. Some content that appears in print may not be available in electronic books. For more information about Wiley products, visit our web site at www.wiley.com.

Library of Congress Cataloging-in-Publication Data

Bergdahl, Michael.
    The ten rules of Sam Walton : success secrets for remarkable results / Michael "Bird Dawg" Bergdahl.
        p.   cm.

    ISBN: 978-0-470-12683-7

    1. Wal-Mart (Firm)—Management.   2. Retail trade—Management.   3. Industrial management.   I. Title: Ten rules of Sam Walton.   II. Title.
    HF5429.215.U6B467   2006
    658.4'09—dc22

                                                                                2005034025

10   9   8   7   6   5   4   3   2   1

To my wife, Sheryl,

my daughter, Heather, and my son, Paul,

who provide the love, support, and

motivation I need to succeed!

Contents

Foreword

Many authors have written books, positive and negative, about the American phenomenon that is Wal-Mart. Michael Bergdahl has an advantage, in that he worked for my father and came to learn many of Dad's lessons about success in business, and in life, from Dad himself.

My father never set out to run the world's largest company. He said many times that he wanted to provide value for customers, create a great workplace for his associates, and be a positive force in the communities we call home. He did so with the values of respect, hard work, continuous improvement, and service, which are as relevant today as they were when he laid them down in the 1960s.

Dad believed strongly in the power of people, so it's fitting that most of his rules for business are really about people, and what can be achieved when you believe in yourself and believe in others. Dad has been gone for more than a dozen years now, but his values live on at the 6,700 stores that serve hundreds of millions of customers every week, all around the world.

As large as Wal-Mart has become, we still find ourselves referring to Dad's "Rules for a Successful Business," embodied in this book.

S. Robson "Rob" Walton
Chairman of the Board,
Wal-Mart Stores, Inc.

Acknowledgments

Special thanks to the following individuals who helped make this book possible:

Sam Fleischman, Literatry Artist Representatives

David Pugh, Senior Editor, John Wiley & Sons, Inc.

Wal-Mart Managers:

> J. Knapp III
> Perry Cheatham
> Frank Baugh
> Randy Smith
> Robert Sauvage
> Andrea Rader

Set High Expectations for Everything You Do

Sam Walton's ability to maintain
the highest standards, while at the
same time getting things done
with lockstep execution, was his secret
for achieving operational excellence.

I'll never forget the first time I met Wal-Mart's founding father, Sam Walton, or Mr. Sam as everyone at Wal-Mart respectfully chose to refer to him. I had arrived in Bentonville, Arkansas, the previous evening and had stayed the night at a Quality Inn, just down the street from Wal-Mart's home office. Bright and early at 7:00 A.M. that Saturday morning I arrived for my interviews with the executive staff of the company. The Wal-Mart executives and headquarters staff all work on Saturday mornings starting at 7:00 A.M. and attend their famous Saturday morning meetings so my arrival for an interview on Saturday fit right into their aggressive work routine. I had three scheduled interviews that day: the first interview with the chief human resources officer, the second with the chief merchandising officer (CMO), and the last with the chief operating officer (COO). As I walked over to my interview with the COO, I remember thinking about a question the CMO had asked me about "what kind of vehicle I drove." Little did I know that when I answered that I drove a pickup truck, I had passed an important Wal-Mart cultural test and that, strangely enough, that answer would be a critical component to my successful interview on that Saturday. You see, Sam Walton, the world's richest man, was known around northwest Arkansas as the billionaire who drove an old red and white 1979 Ford pickup truck. I had passed interview test number one.

At the end of my interview with the COO, I noticed he was looking over my shoulder into the doorway, so naturally I followed his glance and standing in the doorway behind me was an old man wearing coveralls. For just a moment I was under the mistaken impression that this was the janitor who had arrived to pick up the trash that Saturday morning, and then it hit me that this was Sam Walton! I'll never forget the introduction I got to Sam Walton from the COO in his eloquent southern accent. He said, "Mr. Sam, this is Michael Bergdahl." Sam Walton looked at me kind of funny and responded quizzically, "Bird Dawg"? For just a moment, I didn't know whether it was a good thing or a bad thing to be referred to as "Bird Dawg" by Sam Walton. As it turned out, this was good news for me because Sam Walton was a prolific bird hunter who owned several "bird dogs." By the way, the nickname "Bird Dawg" has stuck with me ever since! In that moment when Mr. Sam referred to me as "Bird Dawg," I had become instantaneously endeared to the most successful merchant in the history of the world. I had passed interview test number two.

When I showed up that Saturday, I had no idea that my final interview would be with Sam Walton himself. I later figured out the other executives had prescreened me and had then made the referral to Mr. Sam only after having had a chance to determine that I was qualified for the job. In other words, if I hadn't been qualified for the job, I wouldn't have met Mr. Sam that day at all. I was quite surprised to find that Sam Walton had a down-to-earth, folksy, and disarming personality and for that reason, he was very approachable and easy to talk to. I remember that day he asked me a question about the company I was working for, a question I'll never forget. He said, "Frito-Lay is one of Wal-Mart's largest suppliers and a company I have the greatest respect for. What do you think is the key to their store door delivery system?" At the time it seemed like a harmless question and I remember I told him everything I could about Frito-Lay's state of the art delivery systems. I didn't know it at the time, but Sam Walton was a continuous learner and he used interviews as an opportunity to gather information about other companies, especially his competitors and suppliers. By asking me that question, he was trying to learn about the inner workings of Frito-Lay and without a doubt Sam Walton was searching for a leverage point he could use in price negotiations with them.

I later sat in with him while he interviewed a job candidate from a major grocery store chain in Florida called Publix. This was at a time that Mr. Sam was in the preliminary stages of the Wal-Mart Supercenter strategy. I remember him asking this grocery store manager a familiar question. He said, "Publix is a grocery store chain that I have the greatest respect for. What do you think is the key to their merchandising strategies?" (Mr. Sam later told me that he used interviews as an opportunity to increase his own knowledge of the successful practices of other companies.) After I downloaded all of the secrets I could possibly tell him about the success of Frito-Lay's store door delivery, I had passed interview test number three.

As soon as I met Sam Walton, I respected him immediately and I understood why Wal-Mart's associates referred to him as "Mr. Sam." From that first meeting I could tell that he was a different kind of leader who really cared about people. He had a unique ability to establish rapport, and you could tell he was a down-to-earth and skilled communicator. I came away from that initial interaction knowing I wanted to work with him. On the trip back to my home in Texas that day I was excited about the prospect of working for Wal-Mart, and for the first time I was actually hoping they'd make me a job offer. Later that week I got a phone call offering me the opportunity I was hoping for.

Once I received the official job offer, I was excited and my wife, Sheryl, shared that excitement. Now we were forced to make the most difficult and important decision of our lives. As it turns out, Sheryl was eight months pregnant at the time and the idea of moving from Dallas to Bentonville, so late in her pregnancy, was a real concern. Up to this point, we really hadn't seriously considered the idea of moving to northwest Arkansas, out in the middle of the Ozark Mountains. I had actually been more flattered by the chance to have an interview with the executives of Wal-Mart then I was serious about actually accepting a job if it were offered. In the end, Sheryl and I figured out that moving to Bentonville to work with Sam Walton was the personal and professional adventure of a lifetime. We discussed the opportunity, together with our daughter Heather, and we made the decision to move there so that I could experience Mr. Sam's legendary leadership firsthand. We bought a 17-acre horse farm off a dirt road in the "suburbs" of Bentonville, in a town called Cave Springs. Five days after we arrived, so did our new son Paul, who was born in Rogers, Arkansas, the town where Sam Walton had built his very first discount store.

I was promised I would get the chance to work with Sam Walton and I wasn't disappointed. In my role as the "Director of People" for the home office, I had the chance to work with and around Sam Walton every day. Interestingly, Mr. Sam called his human resources (HR) department "The People Division," which I soon found out was much more than just an interesting name. Fortunately for me, Sam Walton really valued people and he had extremely high standards and high expectations for the people who worked for his company. Over time I found out that it was the people of his organization to whom he credited the phenomenal success of Wal-Mart. My decision to join Wal-Mart had unknowingly put me in the right place at the right time to learn all about Mr. Sam's Golden Rule people philosophies and his success secrets at a pivotal time in his life.

Unintentionally, I became like an embedded reporter, observing Mr. Sam's every move due to my fascination with understanding and learning about his rules for success. At that time I had no plans to write my first book, *What I Learned from Sam Walton: How to Compete and Thrive in a Wal-Mart World* nor did I have a clue I would be writing a second book about his success secrets. As it turns out, I was extremely fortunate to have worked with him in the final years of his life. It was a time when he knew he would soon succumb to bone cancer, yet he continued to work right up to the end of his life. Although it was never said by Mr. Sam, I always felt that in his last years he did everything he could to teach those around him all of his success secrets and philosophies. He inspired everyone around him right up to the very end of his life.

Experiencing Mr Sam's 10 rules for success firsthand has had a profound impact on my approach to my career, my relationships with people, my style of communication, and my personal life. The lessons I learned from him have been internalized over the years, and I have found myself emulating his approach in my dealings with people in business and in life. It is these lessons and examples that I have used in this book to bring his 10 rules for success to life.

As the founder of Wal-Mart* Discount Stores, Wal-Mart Supercenters, and Sam's Club, Sam Walton became the most successful entrepreneur in the history of the world. He was also a self-made man. Starting from scratch, with a singularity of focus, he built the largest and most successful company on Earth. The thing that makes this accomplishment all the more amazing is the fact that he was just a common man who had a vision, set goals, and achieved extraordinary things. The lessons he learned

---

*Throughout this book, "Wal-Mart" includes the various divisions of the company: Wal-Mart Discount Stores, Wal-Mart Supercenters, Sam's Club, Neighborhood Market, Specialty Divisions, Distribution Centers, and home office.

represent a lifetime of focused commitment, risk taking, trial and error, and hard work.

In the final year of his life Mr. Sam wrote down his list of 10 rules for success based on his real world experiences. We are fortunate that by writing down his list of rules, Sam Walton provided us all with the opportunity to learn from his lifetime of experiences, and to implement his formula for success in our own lives. This book is written around Sam Walton's 10 self-professed rules for success. By reading the story behind his rules, you can learn how the world's richest man made his own dreams come true. You can also use things you will learn from his teachings in your own life.

It is important to understand that Mr. Sam set aggressive goals and he believed that it is important to set high expectations in everything you do. For this reason, some of the lessons for success you are about to learn may challenge some of your personal beliefs about what it takes to become successful in business and in life. That's because some of Sam Walton's beliefs challenge conventional wisdom; as he put it, "I swam upstream." He often intentionally avoided the well-worn path in favor of blazing his own trail into uncharted territory. This is actually one of his greatest success secrets.

I will be the first admit that Mr. Sam had an unusually high degree of discipline in his approach to his life and business, so for others to maximize his rules in their own lives will require making a commitment to a higher degree of discipline than some have ever made before. Still others will find they are unwilling to make the commitment necessary to use his rules. Those who are willing and able to internalize his lessons will find themselves achieving success in their personal and professional lives beyond their own expectations. It's exciting to know that you can learn his rules, practice them in your own life, and use them to achieve your true potential. It may be hard to believe, but his simple rules will lead to significant changes in your life if you'll take the time to learn and practice them.

I left Wal-Mart after Sam Walton died and over the years, since working at Wal-Mart's home office, I have often found myself using Mr. Sam's rules in my work and in my personal life. I became a turnaround specialist and coach to businesses and was part of two highly successful business turnarounds in different industries. I've noticed over the years that when I find myself up against a perplexing problem, I often ask myself, "What would Sam do?" Quite often this has worked for me, and I have been successful in solving a problem using the principles and solutions I learned from Mr. Sam himself. The same thing has worked for me in my personal life in my dealings with people in general and in my relationships with my family in particular. I have tried to emulate Mr. Sam's people skills, Golden Rule values, customer service, listening skills, continuous learning, and open communication standards in my own life. In this book, I explain how you can use his rules in your career and in your personal life to help you achieve greater success.

You might be asking yourself, "Why are Sam Walton's 10 rules so important?" My answer to that question is that no one in the history of the world has influenced business practices more than Sam Walton. Just think about the influence he has had on the lives of his customers, suppliers, and associates, not to mention his competitors. His lessons transcend his own company and have changed the way other Fortune 500 companies and their leaders do business. When I worked at Wal-Mart, I often observed the executive teams of some of the most respected companies in the world sitting in as Mr. Sam conducted one of his Saturday morning meetings. The leaders of those great companies were there to learn firsthand about Sam Walton's best practices, and even they wanted to know and use the tools that had made Mr. Sam so successful.

One of the biggest lessons others learned from Mr. Sam was how to treat people, including customers, associates, suppliers, and their fellow human beings. Mr. Sam's rules are influenced by his Golden Rule philosophies, which, simply put, state, "Treat people the way you would want to be treated." His rules are equally important to everyone, including business people, church leaders, athletic coaches, boy scouts, girl scouts, medical professionals, educators, and government employees. If you deal with people, and we all do, Sam Walton's Golden Rule philosophies can help you achieve even greater success professionally, educationally, and in life. Mr. Sam's Golden Rule philosophies are scattered throughout the book.

To know and understand Sam Walton's 10 rules for success, you have to know the story behind how he built his retailing empire. His artistry in building his business masterpiece rivals the brilliance of some of the great accomplishments of mankind. The science behind his success involved challenging existing business theories and current retailing paradigms in search of establishing his own trailblazing best practices. His hard-fought success didn't come easily. The inner demons that drove him were the fear of failure and the belief that good was never good enough. He was so personally motivated, and had such a will to succeed, that he focused on his business almost every waking hour of every day. Sam Walton, the quintessential entrepreneur, once said, "I have always been driven to buck the system, to innovate, to take things beyond where they've been." His goal was to make the consumer number 1 while at the same time treating the associates who worked for him like partners.

Like Michelangelo, Sam Walton's genius materialized out of painstaking trial and error, hard work, long hours, and an insatiable desire to achieve perfection. He was so intense and so determined that everything he did was the best it could be. He was so talented that he reached a pinnacle of artistic genius never before, or since, reached by a man in business; yet, even then he was never completely satisfied with his own work. He's the "Leonardo da Vinci of business innovation," the "Thomas Edison of reinventing business," the "Albert Einstein of business strategy and tactics" all rolled up in one. As a business innovator he was both a continuous learner and continuous change artist who constantly challenged the status quo. He reinvented retailing, merchandising, product purchasing, vendor relationships, expense management, manager/employee relationships, supply-chain retailing technology, and customer service. In his quest to find a better way of doing everything, he would take complex business concepts and simplify them to the point that even complex strategies could be understood and tactically implemented by average people. Some would describe Mr. Sam as a true business genius, whereas others would describe him as simply a very uncommon, common man. Mr. Sam would prefer the latter description!

Sam Walton's background illustrates the painstaking steps he took to become successful. He graduated from the University of Missouri at Columbia with a B.A. in economics. He later served in the military as a captain in the U.S. Army Intelligence Corps. He gained his early retail experience at JC Penney working in Iowa, where he had the chance to work with that company's founder, James Cash "Golden Rule" Penney. It was J.C. Penney who taught Sam Walton the importance of Golden Rule values. Later, Mr. Sam owned and operated a variety store in Newport, Arkansas. With the influence and encouragement of his wife Helen, he opened a five-and-dime on the square in Bentonville, Arkansas, that now serves as the Wal-Mart Visitor's Center, a company historical museum.

Never content, Mr. Sam began to look beyond the small variety store format, and in 1962 opened his first Wal-Mart in Rogers, Arkansas. In the end, his Wal-Mart Discount Stores exceeded everyone's expectations, including his own, resulting in a rapid expansion financed through a public stock offering in 1970. Shareholders, which include most of Wal-Mart's early associates, reaped the benefits of the company's phenomenal success. Over the years patient investors have benefited from 11 two-for-one Wal-Mart stock splits. Many of Mr. Sam's early hourly paid associates who worked for him in the stores and distribution centers or driving trucks retired as millionaires. The wealth of his heirs is estimated in the $100 billion plus range! In recognition of his career accomplishments Sam Walton received honorary doctorate degrees from the University of the Ozarks, University of Arkansas and the University of Missouri. Today, his company has almost 7,000 retail stores around the world.

How did Sam Walton achieve so much? Why were his beliefs so visionary? What is it that made Mr. Sam's style so unique and so successful? Why was he able to fly below the competitive radar? I think the answers to these questions start with the fact that Wal-Mart's humble beginnings were in northwest Arkansas. Nobody really cared because he was plying his trade and testing his ideas in rural America. He perfected his retail strategies and tactics right under the noses of larger competitors who wrote him off as a small-time regional operator. Because he wasn't taken seriously in the early days, he was able to visit many of his competitors and talk directly with their company presidents. He hid his true genius and used his good ole boy, country charm (by saying things like, "I'm just a small-time retailer from Arkansas") to talk his way into meetings with those company's leaders. At that time, it was true that he *was* a small-time operator, but not for long. He was so disarming that they'd willingly share with him the "keys to their kingdom," by telling him the merchandising and operational secrets that had made their own businesses successful. Mr. Sam was "dumb as a fox" as he carefully noted those secrets for his own use later in building his Wal-Mart empire.

When he visited competitor's stores he stalked the aisles in search of product, merchandising, marketing, pricing, employee motivation, and customer service ideas he could use. He didn't waste his time on what others were doing wrong; instead, he'd look for what they were doing right. He believed every company and every individual knew something from which he could learn. He was one of the best listeners you can imagine, and people loved to tell him what they knew. That's why he was always asking questions of everyone he met while he patiently wrote down what he heard. When he discovered a useful idea, he'd take it back, improve upon it, and implement it in his own life or in his business.

Because Sam Walton knew good ideas were everywhere, he believed that at Wal-Mart there is no "extra credit" for coming up with an original idea; an idea is an idea, whether it is internally generated or found externally. By sharing their best practices with Sam Walton, in the long run, as Wal-Mart grew and expanded, some of those competing company leaders had accelerated the failure of their own businesses. They would come to find that it was the information they had so willingly provided to Sam Walton's early development that he later used competitively. In some cases, it may have been the information that those company leaders had provided to Mr. Sam that ultimately led to their own demise!

Learning from what others are doing well is one of the great secrets to Sam Walton's success and one from which all of us can learn. Whether you are a homemaker, college student, professor,

recent graduate, medical professional, federal, state, or local government employee, religious leader, business owner, manager, hourly
paid employee, direct competitor, supplier of Wal-Mart/Sam's Club,
or a current or former Wal-Mart/Sam's Club associate, you can
learn from Mr. Sam's success. Imitation is the sincerest form of
flattery, and as Sam Walton figured out, it is also the quickest way
to self-improvement. My goal in this book, *The Ten Rules of Sam
Walton*, is to give you an insider's perspective into the thought
process behind Mr. Sam's genius. Much of his focus in becoming
successful was on helping those around him to become successful
also. Entwined in each of his rules are recurring themes about
innovation, common sense, hard work, simplification, the power
of positive thinking, and how to treat people. This is why his 10
rules for success are so widely adaptable and applicable for just
about anyone.

In the end, it was Sam Walton's incredible vision and sheer will
and determination that catapulted Wal-Mart to the top of the
Fortune 500. He accomplished his retailing dream through a combination of risk taking, work ethic, innovation, and high expectations. He built the business at a furious pace while simultaneously
conducting his own crude research and development in search of
ways to improve every aspect of his operation. Like building rail-
road track just ahead of a speeding freight train, Sam Walton was
tireless in running his day-to-day operations while trying new
ideas and growing his company at the same time. In his dash for
retailing glory, Mr. Sam ran at a frenetic pace and he had an insatiable desire to live every day to its fullest. He was ever wary of
competitors sneaking up on him from behind, and that thought
alone was enough to fuel and drive his competitive nature. His
singularity of focus, high expectations, stamina, and never-say-die
attitude are the building blocks upon which his company was

built. Current company leaders use that same approach to running the business today, always running at full speed to distance themselves from the rest of their competition.

A lot of Mr. Sam's success was due to the way he treated the people around him. I watched the way he interacted with associates and I was always impressed with the respect and consideration he showed to everyone. One of Wal-Mart's former store managers shared this personal insight about Mr. Sam:

> He was able to make every single associate in that store that he met feel like he was their friend, as well as their boss. He didn't just do it with lip service, he did a lot of things for the associates; he tried to make things better. You were working for a man that you knew truly appreciated you.

Sam Walton's values and beliefs are so important to Wal-Mart that the company still teaches them in its training programs. His autobiography is required reading for newly hired or recently promoted managers. His memory is so revered by the company's leaders and associates that they still refer to him as "Mr. Sam." His beliefs about outthinking, outworking, and outexecuting the competition will remain entangled in the cultural DNA of his company for generations to come. Mr. Sam's legacy is captured in his professed beliefs: "You should set high expectations in everything that you do" and "It's your people who make the difference."

Sam Walton's retailing empire has grown in sales to almost $300 billion. His company has more than 1.7 million associates, more than 6,000 stores across the globe, and more then 120 massive distribution centers. Each week more than 130 million customers cross its thresholds to shop for its everyday low-priced merchandise. Wal-Mart's success is so interwoven into the global economy that when Mr. Sam's giant company projects less than stellar same store sales results, stock markets around the world take a tumble. You might say that when Wal-Mart sneezes, many nations throughout the world, including the United States, catch a cold!

This book is designed to provide the story behind the self-professed rules Sam Walton embraced in order to become successful. Clearly, the rules that Sam Walton followed were the catalyst behind his company's rise from obscurity to world dominance. Because he was just an ordinary man who achieved such extraordinary things, his lessons are easily understood and for that reason are easy for others to replicate in their own lives. The story I have written is the story Mr. Sam would never tell, and I think that is because of his humble nature and his "give credit to everyone else" attitude. You'll soon find that I use great stories to illustrate and bring Mr. Sam's beliefs to life. Some of these stories are from my own firsthand experiences, and others were shared with me by store managers and suppliers who worked directly for and with Sam Walton.

When you boil it all down, much of Wal-Mart's overwhelming success can be credited to Sam Walton's Golden Rule people practices, which are intertwined in the culture he created. He believed in treating people with dignity and respect. He even advertised on his trucks and the walls of his distribution centers and stores the slogan, "Our people make the difference." The cultural attributes responsible for his success were his partnerships with vendors and associates, low resistance to change, sense of urgency, pushing down decision making, simplification of everything, lack of complacency, teamwork, a willingness to act in unconventional ways, and having high expectations. He believed you should follow your passions, believe in yourself, develop and protect your character, and focus on the person in your mirror. He believed that a true leader serves and that we all have the potential to be leaders.

In order to really understand the story of *The Ten Rules of Sam Walton*, you must become familiar with his people practices, in a general and nontechnical way, as they relate to the culture he built at his company. His rules are about strategy, tactics, people, managing expenses, serving others, and taking calculated risks. The life lessons to be learned will prove valuable to anyone interested in reaching his or her full potential.

There is no doubt Sam Walton achieved nothing short of monumental success in business. How did a backwoods retailer accomplish such extraordinary things? What did he discover that others overlooked along the way? How did he come up with so many best practice strategies? What was his roadmap for success? In the end, Sam Walton responded to these kinds of questions in his autobiography by publishing a list of what he considered his 10 most important rules for success. As far as he was concerned, there were 10 key result areas that he considered pivotal to his own success throughout his career. The list below is a summary of Sam Walton's 10 rules. The words that are capitalized are the words Mr. Sam emphasized:

Rule #1 COMMIT to achieving success and always be passionate
Rule #2 SHARE SUCCESS with those who have helped you
Rule #3 MOTIVATE yourself and others to achieve your dreams
Rule #4 COMMUNICATE with people and show you care
Rule #5 APPRECIATE and recognize people for their effort and results
Rule #6 CELEBRATE your own and other's accomplishments
Rule #7 LISTEN to others and learn from their ideas

Rule #8   EXCEED EXPECTATIONS of customers and others
Rule #9   CONTROL EXPENSES and save your way to prosperity
Rule #10 SWIM UPSTREAM, be different, and challenge the status quo

Each of Mr. Sam's 10 rules is easily understandable and can be duplicated by others. But like so many things Sam Walton accomplished, Sam Walton's 10 rules require a high degree of discipline for others to implement. Often it is the breakdown in the tactical execution of strategies, not the strategies themselves, which leads to failures in business and in life. In this book, I have devoted a chapter to each of Mr. Sam's 10 rules. Along the way, I give you the detailed story behind each of Sam Walton's rules so that you can learn from his success and emulate his rules in your own life.

Mr. Sam's rules provide a glimpse into the Wal-Mart playbook and remain a cultural touchstone for the company's leaders to this day. His 10 rules are prominently displayed on a wall for all to see when they arrive in the lobby of the company's headquarters. Many of Wal-Mart's home office associates must walk past this display on the way to their offices each day. Manufacturers and suppliers visiting Wal-Mart's buyers are exposed to Mr. Sam's 10 rules for success every time they visit Wal-Mart's Bentonville home office. The company's executives view Sam Walton's 10 rules as so important they have them displayed on Wal-Mart's web sites in countries around the world.

No matter what you do, this book will provide you with the opportunity to receive personal coaching insights originally developed by the founder of the world's most successful business. I wrote *The Ten Rules of Sam Walton* to tell the story behind Mr.

Sam's success but also to objectively tell the story of his leadership legacy. Although I discuss the company he built throughout this book, the real focus of this story is Wal-Mart's founding father, Sam Walton. Much of what you will read is easy to understand conceptually because Sam Walton was known for keeping things simple. Surprisingly, however, much of what Sam Walton did to make Wal-Mart's Discount Stores, Supercenters and Sam's Club successful is difficult for the undisciplined to replicate; the combination and amount of energy, enthusiasm, and discipline required to succeed is more personal commitment than some people are willing to make. Most people are accustomed to simply picking up the fruit of their labors right off the ground or from the branches within closest reach. Mr. Sam's approach to success requires people to stretch and even climb up into the branches to gather the highest hanging fruit. He had lofty personal and professional goals, and he set high expectations for himself and everyone else around him.

In my first book, *What I Learned from Sam Walton: How to Compete and Thrive in a Wal-Mart World,* I talked about strategies and tactics that retailers, nonretailers, manufacturers, and suppliers can learn from Wal-Mart to compete, survive, and thrive. Since that book was published, I've spoken with people from various organizations and industries at conferences where I was the keynote speaker. What I've found is that there is tremendous interest, domestically and internationally, in learning from and understanding more about how Sam Walton's personality and how his rules contributed to the success of his company. My first book was published and distributed worldwide and has been translated into several languages. Recently, I traveled to Istanbul, Turkey, to speak at a retailing conference and over and over again

I was asked the question, "What is it that makes Wal-Mart…Wal-Mart?" My answer was always the same, "Sam Walton." As a result of that interest, I decided to write my second book about Sam Walton, but this time I am focusing on the rules he felt were most important to his personal success.

Sam Walton's only major mistake, in an otherwise stellar career, may be the fact that he never wrote down the detailed story behind his rules for success. He listed his rules, but never spelled them out in any detail. He gave us a quick glimpse into the "big box," but only a glimpse. I realize he probably didn't share with all of us the details on purpose; just as KFC's Colonel Sanders never shared his original recipe, Mr. Sam gave us a taste of his success strategies but not the step-by-step how-to-do-it formula.

After I talked with some of Wal-Mart's store managers, buyers and suppliers, I decided that there was a great story that needed to be told and that I would flesh out Sam Walton's 10 rules myself. To do so, I interviewed company insiders who worked with and around Sam Walton for many years (most of them, by the way, are financially well off as a result of their own participation in Wal-Mart's lucrative stock programs). I've included the insights they shared with me, along with my own, to provide you with a unique inside perspective on the 10 success secrets of the world's largest and most successful company and its founder. Some of his former associates, who have moved on to other companies, told me they continue to use Mr. Sam's teachings in their business and personal lives to this day. In writing this book I have presented information in such a way that you won't just learn what Mr. Sam's rules are, but, you'll also receive information that you can use to implement his strategies in your own work or in your personal life.

The following chapters will show how Mr. Sam built his business using strategies and tactics he personally developed by learning from experts, observing the best practices of others, and by innovating through trial and error. Regardless of your background, I know you will find these insights helpful as you attempt to prosper and thrive in a Wal-Mart world. You're about to find out why "Setting high expectations really is the key to everything you do" and you'll learn how to use Mr. Sam's rules for success in your own life. Whether you're an entrepreneur, business leader, company manager, supervisor or hourly paid employee, current or former Wal-Mart or Sam's Club associate, educator, student, retiree, homemaker, medical professional, religious leader, law enforcement officer, or government employee, *The Ten Rules of Sam Walton* will provide you with a blueprint for personal success. So here's your chance to learn from the teachings of Mr. Sam himself.

COMMIT to Achieving Success and Always Be Passionate

Sam Walton often went to work
at or before 4:00 in the morning so that
he could review the previous day's
sales reports before the rest of
his executive team arrived!

S am Walton built the largest and most successful company the
world has ever known, and it took a lifetime to do it. His great
accomplishments were achieved because of his ability to maintain
a singularity of focus and his ability to get others motivated to help
him achieve his dream. Think about the challenges facing an entrepreneur like Sam Walton in those early days, out in the middle of
nowhere in the Ozark Mountains, where he opened his first store.
It was 1962 when he founded Wal-Mart, and the first thing his
suppliers told him was that his rural retailing strategies wouldn't
work. Bankers didn't want to help him with loans when he needed
them, believing his venture was destined to fail. Other retailers,
who scoffed at Sam Walton's ideas for rural retailing, were quick
to point out to him there wasn't enough business in rural America
to support a discount retailing venture. Some of the local folks
around northwestern Arkansas must have thought Mr. Sam was
downright crazy to build such big stores in small-town America.
But in the end he proved them all wrong, and it was Mr. Sam, not
his competitors, who had the last laugh!

Mr. Sam may have written his first success secret for achieving
remarkable results, *"COMMIT to achieving success and always be
passionate,"* based on his experiences in those early days when he
first started Wal-Mart. What he lacked in knowledge, skills, and
ability he was able to overcome with his never-say-die determination. His willpower and can-do attitude, coupled with his passion
to succeed, made the difference, early on, during some pretty tough
times. Whether he was born a leader or circumstances made him
become a great leader, the cards he was dealt in the early days of his
entrepreneurial career dictated that he lead by example. His belief
in his dream, his work ethic, and his sheer passion made believers
out of the early associates (the Wal-Mart name for employees) who
helped Sam Walton get his business off the ground. His enthusiasm

for the discount retailing business was infectious, causing those around him to share a similar passion. Mr. Sam would be the first to tell you that it was his associates who were the primary reason Wal-Mart survived those early and difficult first years.

Commitment and passion are two of the most important ingredients necessary for anyone striving to achieve success. It also helps to have a clearly defined vision or goal. Whether you're trying to run a business, raise a family, get a college scholarship, play a musical instrument, or excel in sports, every one of us has to make a personal commitment to achieving success. When the going gets tough, and it always does, it is an individual's passion for his or her goals that gets tested, and often it is that steadfast commitment to succeeding that makes the difference between winning and losing, passing or failing, and success or failure.

J.C. Penney, one of America's retailing pioneers, once said, "Give me someone with no goals and I'll give you a stock clerk. Give me a stock clerk with a goal and I'll give you someone who will make history." Penney's description of the importance of goals to achieving success aptly fits one of his most famous former protégés, Sam Walton. Starting at the bottom and working his way up, Sam Walton learned his craft the hard way by doing every job in a retail store and he learned, under the tutelage of people like J.C. Penney, what it took to be successful. "Golden Rule Penney," as he was called, taught Sam Walton many important lessons about how to treat people that Mr. Sam internalized and which he later passed on to others throughout his life. Sam Walton believed that regardless of the task he was given, if it was worth doing it was worth doing right. He strove to do every job, even the least desirable ones, to the best of his ability. Leading by his own example is just one of the reasons Mr. Sam was so respected and revered by the managers and associates who worked in his company.

In recent years, I've interviewed college seniors for their first jobs following graduation and it has surprised me how many of them stated they wanted to "start at the top!" Of course, that's not possible because it takes years of experience to develop the knowledge and skills necessary to lead an organization effectively. The years of working every kind of job and learning a profession from the bottom up ensure that leaders build their careers on a rock solid foundation of experience. That's what Sam Walton did throughout his career. There wasn't a job in a retail store that Sam Walton hadn't experienced personally. By the way, every one of us who worked with Sam Walton was aware of the fact that he knew more about the inner workings of the business than any of us. His knowledge of the business gave him tremendous credibility, and it also gave those who worked for him confidence in his decision-making ability as a leader.

Mr. Sam had goals and dreams to which he was solidly committed. As a lifelong student he readily accepted guidance, new ideas, and training from others with more experience. He lived his life by setting goals and achieving them, ultimately stair-stepping his way to the very top of the business world. Sam Walton was an example of that stock clerk described by J.C. Penney who made history by committing himself to setting and achieving goals. What was interesting about Mr. Sam's goal orientation is that he approached his business goals sort of like a sports challenge or some kind of contest. He liked to set "stretch" goals so they weren't easy to reach, but at the same time he pursued them with the same enthusiasm and enjoyment he had experienced in sports. He liked to stretch for his personal goals, and he liked to set stretch goals for others in his company. He was motivated to achieve and used goals as a rallying point for everyone around him. He shared his goals with others and had a unique ability as a leader to gain commitment and generate enthusiasm among his associates. Once he got his army of associates committed to achieve a goal, it was truly amazing what his team of average people could accomplish.

Mr. Sam was known for his ability to get above-average performance from a group of average people. Said another way, he had a knack for getting "more from less" from teams of people. By discovering how to achieve "team synergy," he was able to tap into the power of groups of people working together as a team, which is one of the great secrets to how Mr. Sam achieved such unbelievable results at Wal-Mart. Sam Walton believed that in business and sports, it is teams of committed people working together towards a common goal that win, not individuals working separately.

Mr. Sam was more than a little embarrassed when he confessed that there wasn't a day that went by in his adult life that he didn't ponder some aspect of his business. In his quiet moments, he was constantly "noodling" the product mix or how to display products to sell more at a higher velocity or thinking of ways to improve customer service. I can picture him sitting there, on a Sunday afternoon "relaxing" on his porch swing at his home, legal pad and pen in hand, enjoying the mental exercise of how to improve product distribution, reduce costs, improve associate relations, or lower prices. Although he was a family man, he was also a merchant who was committed to doing whatever was necessary to make his business successful.

Sam Walton built Wal-Mart and Sam's Club with his singularity of focus. He created a vision, set goals, and got others excited about achieving those goals. He was a passionate and committed leader who inspired a similar level of passion and commitment in others. Throughout his life he heard many a naysayer telling him that this idea he had or that idea he had wasn't going to work. Sometimes those naysayers were right, but more often than not it was Mr. Sam who proved them wrong. He remained determined and committed to his dream of making Wal-Mart the best company in retail until the day he died. One of the most important lessons each of us can learn from Sam Walton is that if you are willing to focus on your goals and personally remain committed to do whatever is necessary to achieve them, you will be successful.

I read an interesting story written by the motivational expert Earl Nightingale called *The Strangest Secret*. In that story he describes the key to success in business and in life. When I deliver speeches domestically and internationally I often ask my audiences to raise their hand if they are interested in knowing what The Strangest Secret is? Almost everyone in the audience enthusiastically raises their hand, and here is what I share with them. The key to being successful at whatever you want to accomplish in life is "What you think about most of the time is what you become." If you think about achieving your goals and put your time, energy, and effort behind achieving them, what you think about most of the time is what you will become.

If you have a goal to be the best athlete, medical professional, parent, or business leader, take the time to figure out how to overcome the obstacles, and are willing to learn the necessary skills you need to achieve that goal, you will in all likelihood become successful. If you want to become a great golfer, you have to think and dream about becoming a great player and you've got to practice, practice, and practice some more. If you want to become a great doctor, you have to focus your energies on becoming the best in your profession. If your goal is to raise well-adjusted children, you have to focus on nurturing your kids. If you are Sam Walton and you want to build the greatest retail organization in the history of the world, you have to think about achieving that goal morning, noon, and night. That's exactly what Sam Walton did to make Wal-Mart so successful. Always remember, what you think about most of the time is what you will become. I personally think Earl Nightingale's *The Strangest Secret* should really be called life's *Greatest Success Secret*. Think about what might be achieved in our society if parents and educators taught every school-age child this lesson. Just imagine what might be accomplished by those children when they become adults!

The success achieved by Sam Walton didn't come easily, and he was by no means an overnight success. He learned his craft the hard way over his entire lifetime by committing himself to painstakingly learn every aspect of his business. He was a generalist not a specialist, and he valued people who were willing to roll up their sleeves to do whatever it took to move the business forward. He expected his home office corporate associates from every department to have a broad and comprehensive understanding of the business and a specific point of view on the real issues affecting the company's success. He required everyone who worked at Wal-Mart to think and act like a retail merchant. Mr. Sam expected everyone around him to share the same focus, passion, and commitment for retailing that he did.

He valued team results more than individual results. His professed philosophy at Wal-Mart for winning in business was "teams win, not individuals!" Interestingly enough, because of Mr. Sam's charismatic leadership, the vast majority of his associates shared his "Teams win" philosophy and his associates enthusiastically worked together to beat Wal-Mart's competition.

Often the leaders of organizations have difficulty getting others to share their enthusiasm for achieving organizational goals. Athletic coaches, church leaders, and business leaders experience the same kinds of challenges as they attempt to get their team, their flock, or their company to share their excitement for achieving goals. Sometimes this happens because those leaders have set goals in a vacuum without involving the entire team. People lack enthusiasm for goals that they perceive as unrealistic so it is important to get people involved in the goal-setting process so that they perceive the final performance targets as achievable. One of the ways Sam Walton gained commitment from his team was by getting everyone involved in providing input as the goals were being set. In the process, he gained their commitment or what Mr. Sam referred to as "ownership." He figured out that people who are involved in setting goals have a tendency to set goals higher than their leaders would have set them, and because of that feeling of ownership they do whatever is necessary to achieve them.

Sam Walton had three very important cultural goals for the associates who worked for his company. The first is that he strove to hire the best-quality people that he could possibly find. Second, he was committed to providing the best training and development for his associates. Finally, he wanted his stores to be the best places to work. Because of the limited pool of people available to work in his retail stores, Sam Walton often hired inexperienced people who demonstrated enthusiasm, a good attitude, and good interpersonal skills. He proved you can take unskilled people with potential and teach them what they need to know to do their jobs.

It wasn't unusual for Mr. Sam to shift people around into new jobs, for which they had no prior experience, in order to facilitate cross-training. Keep in mind that the people he hired in the early days were right off the farms of northwestern Arkansas, eastern Oklahoma, southeastern Kansas, and southern Missouri. Like Mr. Sam, they were common, ordinary people with an uncommon commitment to succeed. By giving them a job and an opportunity, his early associates proved they were equal to his trust, and they reciprocated by giving him their undying loyalty. Mr. Sam's inspirational leadership remains the standard by which other Wal-Mart and Sam's Club leaders are measured to this day.

I was shocked and surprised when I first joined Wal-Mart to realize that a large number of associates were hired from the farm communities around northwestern Arkansas. Most did not have the college education that is a standard prerequisite for getting hired at other large corporations. Mr. Sam would hire the inexperienced and place them in highly responsible professional positions across every functional area in his home office. Mr. Sam liked the idea of growing his own people by allowing them to learn on the job. It was quite normal for him to hire or promote people into professional positions for which they had no experience. The thing I found the most astounding was how Sam Walton turned a team of average people into high performers. I asked one of Wal-Mart's former store managers to explain this strategy to me and here is what he told me:

> Mr. Sam had a way of taking average people and turning them into above average performers. I think that is reflected in the fact that you have so many people that come on board that are just "average Joes" off the street and then look at them 7, 8, or 10 years later and see what they are doing with the company. It comes from, I think, basics. First of all you make them partners and you share as much information with them as you possibly can. You operate on the premise that everybody wants to be successful. So your job as a store manager, assistant manager or department manager is not to browbeat somebody and beat them up, your job is to operate on the premise that they want to be successful; what do I need to do to help them to be successful. If somebody is falling short, Wal-Mart doesn't write them off and get rid of them and say

bring me somebody else. Wal-Mart's leaders say wait a minute, this associate wants to do a good job and something is keeping them from doing a good job and what is it? They ask what roadblock is in the way, what hurdle can I help them get over so that they can do a good job? Wal-Mart will exhaust that train of thought before they will ever let anybody go. That's what Wal-Mart's coaching process is all about; it's not a discipline process, it's a process of making someone successful. When you have that mentality where you are treated like a partner and the entire focus of the organization is to help you to be successful, I really think it changes the dynamics of the people part of the business.

To this day, the company's leaders inspire ordinary people around the world to achieve at very high levels. The fact that the company has been so wildly successful with this staffing strategy is one of the greatest testaments to Sam Walton's leadership philosophies. I've worked for other companies and none of them intentionally go out of their way to hire average or ordinary people; in fact, almost all company leaders will proudly tell you that they hire above-average or extraordinary people. Unfortunately, the result of their efforts in many cases is a group of highly paid, above-average employees who are performing at average levels; they "get less from more." One of the great secrets of Wal-Mart's success is its ability to take average people with good attitudes, teach them the skills they need to turn them into high performers, and in the end "get more from less."

Mr. Sam liked promoting inexperienced people from within and giving them a chance to succeed with the full knowledge that he was throwing them in over their heads; he called it "picking 'em green." Mr. Sam's belief in people created a self-fulfilling prophecy of success. His staffing strategy was one part inspiration and one part perspiration. His trust and belief in people provided all the inspiration they needed. The perspiration came from their fear of failure and their fear of possibly letting Mr. Sam down, which drove them to do whatever it took to succeed. What they lacked in knowledge, skills, and ability they made up for in passion, long hours, and hard work. To this day, Mr. Sam's staffing legacy continues around the world, with an estimated 75 percent of all management positions at Wal-Mart being filled via promoting associates from within who have demonstrated a good attitude, people skills, and work ethic.

With so many inexperienced people getting promoted into leadership positions you'd be right if you assumed that some of them failed. When they didn't succeed. Sam Walton did something unusual in businesses today; he would move them back into a lower position with less responsibility. Having worked in human resources for over 25 years, I had been trained to believe that demoting employees to lower positions and lower pay levels is a recipe for disaster. In society there is a negative stigma attached to demotions. It's a sign of failure and an indication that the individual who was demoted just wasn't good enough. That's not the case at Wal-Mart. Out of necessity, Mr. Sam was forced to promote people to higher levels of responsibility before they were ready. It happened every day and still happens every day around the world. Most of the time those who were "picked green" were so passionate and committed to succeed that they were able to make up for their shortcomings and do what was necessary to become successful. Sometimes those promoted too early would fail and would have to "step down" (a Wal-Mart term for a demotion), but 8 or 9 out of 10 times those who were promoted from within did succeed.

I met associates at the Wal-Mart home office who had been promoted several times and then demoted, more than once! At

Wal-Mart, unlike most corporations, there is no badge of dishonor, shame, or stigma attached to being demoted or "stepping down." Everyone seemed to understand that when you promote so many "green" associates, every once in a while someone won't be equal to the challenge and will have to step down. The thing that amazes me is how seldom demotions actually occurred, and I think that's because, as Mr. Sam put it, "Our people want to win so badly they just go out there and they get it done, even though some believe they can't succeed."

I think Mr. Sam figured out that people are hungry for responsibility and want to prove to themselves and others that they are equal to the challenge. He realized that everyone has withheld potential and if a leader will simply give people a chance to succeed, they will do whatever is necessary to prove they can be successful. Human nature is such that most people want the chance to prove they are capable of handling more responsibility. Once Mr. Sam gave people leadership responsibilities, I believe some of those who were promoted actually drove themselves to succeed because they didn't want to let him down.

There is a lesson all leaders can learn from Mr. Sam's experiences in promoting people from within at Wal-Mart: Give people responsibility before you think they are ready. If an individual has good people skills and a strong work ethic and demonstrates a willingness to learn, why not give them a chance to develop their leadership skills in a position of greater authority? As a leader, you'll find that people will rarely let you down if you give them a chance to achieve their full potential. Sometimes an experienced individual who has done it all before won't do as good a job over the long haul as a less experienced individual who is promoted to greater responsibilities and is hungry to prove that he or she is equal to the challenge.

One of the reasons Mr. Sam had so many successes when he promoted inexperienced people was because he created a positive self-fulfilling prophecy; in other words, he believed in people more than they believed in themselves. By doing so he provided the backbone or support many people seem to need to reach their full potential. I think Sam Walton believed in the potential of ordinary people more than they believed in their own ability. His approach was really quite simple. Find people with a good attitude and they'll do what they have to do to be successful. He didn't care if the people he promoted were old, young, male, female, black, brown, or white. It didn't matter to Mr. Sam because he was promoting talented people who he sensed had raw potential and who were passionate. He tapped into a pool of dedicated people who had drive and a good outlook because he knew he could teach them everything else. He acted as a catalyst and he inspired them to accomplish more then they thought could. His inspiration gave them all the confidence they needed to achieve. As was always the case with Mr. Sam, he didn't take credit when those he promoted were successful, but instead he attributed the success of his associates to their own strong desire to be successful and to win.

Leaders at most organizations don't move people into a new leadership role as aggressively as Mr. Sam did, and many of them will tell you that at their organization promoting inexperienced people just won't work. Mr. Sam often challenged the conventional wisdom of "the way things are done" in the world. Leaders at other organizations have rejected some of his best ideas and have held to the tried and true, more conventional leadership methods. Mr. Sam believed the greatest opportunities are often found by trying new and unconventional ways of doing things and by rejecting conventional wisdom. He enjoyed blazing new trails and he believed that's where you find the competitive advantage. In reality, the only reason Wal-Mart's cross-training and picking 'em green strategies won't work in other organizations is because of the self-fulfilling belief on the part of their leaders that they won't! As in this staffing example, Mr. Sam was a "paradigm buster."

A paradigm is a commonly held belief that people use as a filter for evaluating new information. In life a paradigm is often the tried and true way of doing things; it's the conventional wisdom or the way everybody else does it. We all have paradigms or commonly held beliefs in every area and aspect of our lives. Sometimes those paradigms enable us to succeed and other times they disable us, hold us back, and relegate us to mediocrity.

As an illustration, here's an example of a simple geographic paradigm shared by many people. If I told you Reno, Nevada, is west of San Diego, California, I think many would agree that this is not true. Your geographic paradigm tells you that anything west of San Diego is out in the ocean. But the fact is that Reno, Nevada, is west of San Diego, California. When confronted with information like this that challenges our existing beliefs or paradigms, many people will reject the new information even when they intellectually know the new information is true. Some will go to an atlas or globe more to prove that their belief is the correct one than to verify that the new information is accurate. Even when the facts have been proven beyond a shadow of a doubt, some will become confused or perplexed by new information that is contrary to their existing beliefs. In some cases, individuals will reject the new factual information outright.

Paradigms are powerful because they represent our perceptions of reality, and sometimes people cling to their perceptions even when they know they are wrong. This is one of the reasons that change is so difficult for people to accept. Sam Walton embraced change as a welcomed friend, and he truly was a paradigm buster who was committed to challenging the conventional wisdom. The last thing you'd ever want to tell Sam Walton, as the reason he should do something a certain way, was because that's the way everyone else does it. Faced with this logic, you could bet Mr. Sam would go in the opposite direction and try to find his own different and unique "Wal-Mart Way."

I learned a valuable lesson from Mr. Sam that every leader needs to know about the acceptance of change by people. When getting people to understand the reasons behind the change, don't focus on getting them to agree with the change. The reality is that it's not necessary for everyone faced with a change to agree with the change, but they do need to understand the reasons behind the change and commit to implementing it. When a leader seeks to get people to understand the reasons behind the change and stops trying to gain agreement, change occurs more rapidly. Organizationally, people can agree to disagree with a change, but they must understand the change and adapt to it or face the consequences. Mr. Sam was a master communicator, and this is the approach I saw him use successfully when he was faced with implementing small and large changes of direction.

Early on, Mr. Sam established a set of values to which he remained committed throughout his career. He valued things like growth and development of his associates, service to his customers, treating people the way he would want to be treated, quality in everything he did, professionalism and ethics in his actions, competitiveness and a will to win, continuous learning, and continuous productivity improvement. I was reminded of one or more of these beliefs every time I was around Mr. Sam.

I remember watching and listening to him interact with college interns who were working for the company during the summer, and I was struck by the sincerity of his interest in their education, careers, and families. It was clear to me that he treated people the way that he himself wanted to be treated. He maintained those same Golden Rule values from the time he started Wal-Mart until the end of his life. Wal-Mart's leaders remain committed to these same values to this day. Over the years, I have found myself using many of Mr. Sam's Golden Rule values in my own work and personal life.

Mr. Sam valued the people around him. For this reason he believed in going out of his way to interact with his associates, customers, suppliers, and Wal-Mart's shareholders. Because he was a pilot, Mr. Sam flew out in his own plane almost every week of the year to visit people in his stores. I remember trying to set up a meeting with Mr. Sam and being warned by his administrative assistant that he was tough to pin down for scheduled meetings because he might decide to jump in his plane and fly out to the stores with little or no prior notice. When the company was smaller, he set a goal to personally visit every single store every year; this goal quickly became unachievable as the number of store locations grew into the thousands. He was famous for arriving at a store unannounced and for walking around talking to customers and associates, who found him both approachable and easy to talk to.

Sam Walton picked up many of his best ideas from his competitors by visiting their stores as he flew around the country and observing firsthand their customer service, product selection, and merchandising practices. In the early days, he'd often set up meetings with the presidents of other retail companies to discuss the strategies that he had already observed on his visits to their stores. He was an innovator, but he wasn't afraid to imitate the successful strategies of others. In fact, his ultimate success was a result of a lifetime of imitation and innovation. He was an incessant learner who was never satisfied with business as usual. Good was never good enough for Sam Walton because he was always in search of a better way.

There was little luck involved in his creation of Wal-Mart; his success was one part vision, one part singularity of focus, and one part hard work. His quest for success represented a lifelong commitment to achieving excellence. Mr. Sam would be the first to admit that Wal-Mart's success far exceeded any expectation he had for the business. His goal was never to make Wal-Mart the biggest company in the world; his dream was to make it the best. He always told everyone that Wal-Mart's success was more a result of the efforts and contributions of his associates rather than anything he himself had done. In the final analysis, Wal-Mart's success can be directly attributed to its founder and those early associates who were committed to his rural discount retailing strategy, something that had never been done before. Mr. Sam's willingness to keep going in those difficult early years, under withering criticism, is a testament to his unwavering commitment, passion, and vision. His fanaticism for Wal-Mart inspired others around him to share his dream.

Robert Greenleaf, a noted management expert, said, "Not much happens without a dream. And for something great to happen, there must be a great dream. Much more than a dreamer is required to bring it to reality; but the dream must be there first." Sam Walton had a dream of turning Wal-Mart into the best retailing establishment in the world and that's precisely what it has become. Along the way he also became the most successful merchant the world has ever seen. He did it the hard way by painstakingly outthinking, outworking, outplanning, and outexecuting his competitors. In the process, his company became the best retailer in America and the biggest company on earth. Over the years, Sam Walton received a variety of awards and recognition, but being named "America's Most Successful Merchant," in a Fortune magazine cover story was one of his career highlights.

As I've read about and studied successful people, such as entrepreneurs, company founders, business leaders, athletic coaches, educators, political leaders, and religious leaders, I've found they all seem to share this same singularity of focus. They have an idea or a dream and they are passionate about it. They are willing to do whatever is necessary to make that dream come true. They remain committed even when their ideas fly in the face of conventional wisdom. They develop an uncanny ability to focus, even when they are told by others that their ideas won't work; they remain committed to their dreams when most would have walked away. It is that same commitment that separates the great coach, minister, or educator from the not so good, the best accountants from the average accountants, the great sales and service people from the poor ones, the high-performing hourly wage employee who makes a difference from the one who just goes through the motions, and the great nurses or the best students or the terrific government workers from the ones who obviously don't care. Commitment is a choice. You're not born with it; everyone has an equal opportunity to make a commitment to achieve their full potential and to be the best that they can be.

As an example, I remember sitting in Carnegie Music Hall watching my daughter, Heather, play viola in the symphony orchestra. As I sat there, I reminisced about all the years of private lessons she had to endure and the personal sacrifices she made to allow her to become a talented musician. She dedicated herself to hours and hours of practice. She was committed to her dreams, and the result was the opportunity to perform before large audiences in great concert halls. As I watched and listened that day, I realized that her great accomplishment in music was a direct result of her vision, self-sacrifice, discipline, and dedication. Luck wasn't a contributing factor. Her hard work and commitment to her goals had provided her with the opportunity to achieve great things musically, at the highest level. It's that same kind of passionate determination that is required to succeed in any worthwhile endeavor.

Every day that Sam Walton's leadership team steps onto the competitive playing field they do so with that same kind of passion and commitment. They know they will do what's necessary to outperform the competition. I feel that often the difference between success and failure in sports, business, and in life is starting with the commitment and belief that you will be successful in the first place. Mr. Sam's beliefs about achieving success are captured nicely in this quote by Calvin Coolidge: "Nothing in the world can take the place of persistence. Talent will not; nothing is more common than unsuccessful men with talent. Genius will not; unrewarded genius is almost a proverb. Education will not; the world is full of educated derelicts. Persistence and determination alone are omnipotent." Mr. Sam lived his life this way and he taught his associates to make a difference each and every day.

Regardless of what you want to achieve in life your ultimate success or failure will be influenced by your beliefs and attitudes as you begin. If you think you'll succeed, you probably will, and if you think you'll fail, you will probably fail. There is power in positive thinking and you have to start with the end in mind, believing you will be successful. Positive thoughts lead to positive outcomes, and negative thoughts lead to negative outcomes; it's as simple as that. There was never a doubt in Sam Walton's mind that he would be successful no matter what he did. Challenge yourself to be the best you can be and always maintain a positive outlook and you'll find yourself accomplishing more than you ever thought possible.

The spirit in which Sam Walton conveyed his leadership values to the rest of his team is best exemplified when he said:

> Our method of success, as I see it, is Action with a capital A, and a lot of hard work mixed in. We've said it through the years: Do it. Try it. Fix it. Not a bad approach and it works. There are a lot of people out there who have some great ideas, but nothing in the world is cheaper than a good idea without any action behind it. We must be action-oriented doers. It's a whole lot more fun, and accomplishes so much more.

Just like Sam Walton's success, the single most important element to your success is to do something every day that moves you in the direction of your goals. The longest journey begins with the first step, and once you finally commit yourself you must keep taking steps in the direction of your goal. Success is not a result of a serendipitous event, chance, or luck. It is a product of your never-ending hard work and erring on the side of action. The key to success I learned from Sam Walton is to do something each and every day to move yourself in the direction of achieving your goals. If you'll break your goals down into a logical progression of steps, it makes focusing on achievement of the overall goal much easier. I heard it put this way: "Inch by inch everything's a cinch, but yard by yard everything is hard!" There is also a feeling of satisfaction along the way as you stair-step your way to accomplishing your goal.

You make yourself successful by having a good idea, focusing on bringing it to fruition, and then staying the course. Regardless of what you do in life, the same lessons about hard work and commitment hold true for everyone. The success formula is quite simple: stick to what you believe, take calculated risks, focus on your goals, and do something every day to make your goals reality. If you maintain this level of commitment, what you think about most of the time is what you will become.

Let me give you an example. When I was a freshman in college, I tried out for the soccer team. My goal was simply to make the team. I remember that there were many freshmen trying to make the team that year and that I was going to need to set myself apart if I hoped to get one of the few slots available to freshmen that year.

My strategy from day one was to outwork and outperform my fellow competitors. Here's what I did. At the beginning of every practice our coach, who was a real stickler for fitness, made us run 10 laps around the field as a warm-up. The distance was about 2½ miles. I decided from the very first practice that I would run those laps harder than anyone else. Picture 25 players jogging those laps clumped together and one player running those laps and breaking away from the pack. That was me. Each day my goal was to run fast enough to lap the entire team before I completed the 10 laps. My coach took notice from the very first practice. I continued to lap the team at every practice and when the coach later announced which freshmen had made the team, I was one of them. Not only did I make the team but I was named one of the starters in every game my freshman year. The next season the coach named me captain of the team. My commitment to making the team is truly an example of what I thought about most of the time is what I had become. Success in business and in life is about attitude and choices. You can make the choice to be the best, or you can choose to be part of the pack. The choice is yours.

Let me share a story with you about Sam Walton's commitment to success. When I headed Wal-Mart's home office "people division" staff, as the Director of Human Resources, I had a chance to experience Mr. Sam's leadership and work ethic firsthand. One Sunday morning, I arrived at the home office bright and early to conduct a job interview with an out-of-town recruit who I had just picked up from the Bentonville Quality Inn, where he was staying. As we made our way into the executive office area, for his first interview at 7:00 A.M., we passed by Mr. Sam's office and much to my surprise, there he was at his desk. After dropping the recruit off for his first interview, I went back to see what Sam Walton was up to; I asked him what he was doing at his office on a Sunday morning at 7:00 A.M., and then I asked him what time he had arrived. As it turns out, Sam Walton had shown up for work that Sunday morning at 4:00 A.M., and the reason he was there stunned me. He said that by arriving at work so early in the morning he was able to get *real work* done. During the week, he was thrust into a whirlwind of meetings and store visits, leaving him little time to get his thoughts organized to think of ways to improve the business. He lamented that as the company had become more and more successful, he had less and less time to himself. He had also become a bit of a celebrity in his own right and was pestered for autographs and pictures everywhere he went. He said he enjoyed the opportunity for private, uninterrupted time before the rest of the staff arrived each morning to gather his thoughts for the day ahead. Mr. Sam said that he would come to work most days of the week at 3:00 or 4:00 A.M. to get a head start on everybody else by reviewing the sales reports from the previous day.

Wal-Mart's executives weren't sleeping in either; some of them started arriving for work as early as 5:00 A.M. The work ethic of Wal-Mart's management is one of the company's great competitive advantages. Think about this: While East Coast retail executives were still sleeping, Sam Walton was at his desk working each and every day. As the rest of his executives were arriving at 5:00 A.M., CST, most East Coast executives were just getting out of bed. By the time most of the executives of Wal-Mart's competitors reach their offices and get their first cup of coffee of the day at 9:00 A.M. EST, the Bentonville managers have already been working at their desks or have been in meetings for two, three, or possibly four hours. As West Coast retailers are leaving their offices at 5:00 P.M.

PST, some of those same Bentonville executives are still working and will continue working until 8:00 or 9:00 P.M. CST. The commitment and sacrifice Wal-Mart's leaders make on behalf of their beloved company is like none other I have ever seen. Many of the company's home office executives and its managers in the distribution centers and stores work a 75- to 90-hour work week and more! With a global operation crossing every time zone on the planet, the pressure to execute around the world pushes committed leaders to "take one for the team" by working whatever hours are necessary just to keep up with the volume of work. The commitment Wal-Mart's leaders have today is the same commitment Sam Walton had over 40 years ago when he opened his first store.

I would experience this work ethic firsthand at Wal-Mart's Bentonville home office. I would arrive for work at 7:00 in the morning and because I arrived so "late," I was forced to park 8 or 10 rows back in the parking lot. As I'd walk into the building, I'd pass the cars of those who had arrived earlier than I had. I'd often see the same vehicles in the rows closest to the building. Of course, Mr. Sam's pickup truck was there in the row closest to the building. Most of those same cars were still there when I'd leave at 6:30 or 7:00 at night. The work ethic of the people I met at Wal-Mart was unlike any I had ever experienced before or since.

The work ethic of Sam Walton is legendary. His philosophy for success was, "Early to bed and early to rise makes a man (or woman) healthy wealthy and wise!" I later adopted the same strategy in my own life and I often get up at 4:00 in the morning to begin my work day. I find working in the early morning is a great way to get out ahead of my work for the day with no interruptions. If it worked for Mr. Sam, I figured it would work for me. The people who work at Wal-Mart share Mr. Sam's work ethic. When I worked there I noted that the company's managers were willing to work whatever hours were necessary to get their work done. I never worked for a company that had as much work to get done as there is at Wal-Mart. I can tell you that there was never a day I can remember when I left in the evening with all my work done. It was impossible to get it all done, and I think that was part of Mr. Sam's plan to keep all of us challenged every day! I can tell you that working under that kind of work load is stressful for those of us who like to get everything done, every day.

Like all of Sam Walton's 10 rules, "COMMIT to achieving success and always be passionate" is still aggressively practiced by Wal-Mart's leaders. Current executives admit they still arrive at work at 6:00 or 6:30 A.M. each day, many still travel to the stores every week of the year, and they still conduct Saturday morning strategy and tactics meetings attended by all of the top leaders of the company. They still shop their own stores, and they shop the stores of their competitors. In their enthusiasm to compete and win, they continue to live Mr. Sam's example by outworking the competition.

I have been asked over the years, by people who were interested in going to work for Wal-Mart, if I thought they should go to work there. I tell them, "If you are a team player who is willing to work harder than you have ever worked before and are willing to dedicate yourself to the success of the company, you won't find another organization that offers more opportunity." But I also point out that if they do go to work at Wal-Mart, maintaining a balance between working there and one's personal life is the most difficult issue an individual or family will face. The incredible commitment required to work for Wal-Mart is not for everyone, but I tell them that they will never work with a more dedicated team of people. Most who go to work for the company adapt to its aggressive culture, but some simply can't.

Prior to joining Wal-Mart I had worked for other demanding companies, including a publishing business owned by my wife's family. I had been born with a strong work ethic so I thought adapting to Wal-Mart's aggressive work standards would be an easy transition, but it wasn't. The time commitment demanded by Sam Walton was truly extraordinary. He led by his own example, and the rest of the leadership team willingly followed. I worked harder and longer hours than I had ever worked before. Because of Mr. Sam's lean staffing strategies I was stretched and challenged to achieve more than I thought was possible, but with the help of those around me I figured out, just like everybody else, how to get the most important tasks completed each day.

Now that you have a sense of Sam Walton's philosophies, let me ask you a question. Are you willing to pay the price in time, energy, and effort and make the personal sacrifices necessary to be successful? The fact is that you have to be committed if you expect to achieve your goals or if you expect others around you to share your commitment. As a leader, if you are willing to lead by example, you will send a powerful message about your work ethic, standards, and commitment. "What you do speaks much louder than what you say." At Wal-Mart, Sam Walton called it "walking the talk."

Sam Walton never asked anyone to do anything that he wasn't willing and able to do himself. He believed that you have to set high standards for your own performance if you expect to hold others to high standards. By demonstrating his willingness to work long hours and travel to his stores and distribution centers to speak with customers and associates directly, he sent powerful cultural expectation messages to everyone on his team. The standards he lived by have become the standards by which current and future generations of Wal-Mart leaders are measured.

Along the way, Mr. Sam threw himself into his work 100 percent. The decisions he made required personal sacrifice, including time away from his wife and children. The support of his wife Helen was pivotal to his ability to focus on the business. He was fortunate to have a wife like Helen Walton who was willing to raise the family, thus giving him the freedom he needed to pursue his dreams. The company that Sam Walton built would not be what it is today without the emotional support provided to him by Helen Walton.

Not everyone has a spouse who is willing to make the sacrifices and provide the support for his or her dreams to the degree Helen Walton did for Sam Walton. In the early days, she was instrumental in securing financing from her father at a time when Mr. Sam had difficulty getting cash from banks. Sam Walton may be the founding father of Wal-Mart, but it is Helen Walton who supported him throughout his career, giving him the opportunity he needed to focus his energy on making Wal-Mart such a great success; without her support, who knows what could or would have happened?

As in Sam Walton's personal example, achieving success in business or in any other walk of life requires paying the price. There is no easy path to success. If you aren't willing to work hard or if you're not willing to put in the hours necessary to be successful, you'll find the path to achieving your goals extremely difficult. Unfortunately, hard work alone is no guarantee. Like Sam Walton you have to have a good idea, believe in it wholeheartedly, and doggedly pursue it. That's the Sam Walton and Wal-Mart way. You can have the best idea or business concept ever imagined, but without the effort behind it nothing will happen. There's a perfect phrase comprised of 10 two-letter words which I think summarizes the way Sam Walton viewed his personal commitment to achieving his dreams: If it is to be it is up to me!

Read and reread this phrase and internalize it into your own personal success strategy for your work and for your life. I believe it is so important to success that I have repeated this phrase to my son Paul, my daughter Heather, and my nephews Ross and RJ over the years in the hope that they will internalize and embrace this philosophy themselves as they face the challenges ahead. Contained within this phrase is one of the most important and powerful lessons to achieving the proper level of personal commitment in everything you do—athletically, educationally, emotionally, socially, or spiritually—not just in pursuit of your business or career. Whenever you are looking for the answer to solve your problems, often that answer rests within you. Do something each and every day to move a step closer toward the achievement of your goals. No matter what you want to accomplish, you can do it if you'll personally embrace the belief "If it is to be it is up to me!"

Sam Walton always had a positive can-do attitude; it was as if he viewed the world through rose-colored glasses. He created his own positive self-fulfilling prophecies by believing that you reap what you sow. If you think in negative terms, you will get negative results; if you think in positive terms, you will more than likely get positive results. Mr. Sam didn't have much patience for pessimistic people who acted like they were defeated before they ever got started. He believed that those who say they can't do something are actually saying, "I won't try." Mr. Sam was optimism personified, and he was confident he could achieve anything he set his mind to. His formula for success was belief plus effort equals results. He believed negativity and lack of belief, coupled with a lack of effort, was the sure path to failure. In Sam Walton's world, people who think that way "need to get out of the way of those who are doing it!" Winston Churchill captured the essence of Mr. Sam's belief when he said, "A pessimist sees the difficulty in every opportunity; an optimist sees the opportunity in every difficulty." Sam Walton, the eternal optimist, was quick to correct those who used the term "problem" in describing a challenge they were facing by telling them the Wal-Mart and Sam Walton Way is to refer to "problems" as "opportunities."

Sam Walton was a continuous learner who believed in continuously improving every area of his operation. I believe his dedication to the pursuit of excellence may stem from his experiences playing football in high school and college. To become the best you can be in any athletic endeavor, you have to focus, work out, practice specific skills, and often even modify your diet. You have to be willing to dedicate yourself to achieving excellence. In a word, success takes discipline. To become a peak performer, you have to train your body and train your mind. You have to find and create your own competitive edge as you overcome any God-given limitations you may have, or leverage the gifts you've received. In terms of sports, Sam Walton wasn't a big man, but he dedicated himself to being the best that he could be, and by working hard he willed himself to become a great athlete. Mr. Sam was one of the most competitive people you'll ever meet, and he encouraged that same desire in Wal-Mart's executives, managers, and associates to compete and win.

Early on in his career, Mr. Sam could probably have been accused of working hard and not smart. When faced with a challenge, he believed in erring on the side of action rather than inaction. What he was missing in knowledge and strategy he'd make up in hard work and execution. Fortunately, he hired great strategists and planners once he got the business off the ground. Most small business owners can relate to Sam Walton's bent towards action. Like Mr. Sam, that "ready, shoot, aim" approach is how many people run their businesses and their lives; when in doubt, they err on the side of action and do something to move forward. Lacking a clearly defined strategy, many people use that approach throughout their lives and in the end they wonder why they haven't accomplished more. If you are one of those people who lack a plan, take the time to write your goals down on paper and you'll find your chances of accomplishing them will increase. If you don't, you're living the definition of business insanity, which is doing things the way you've always done them and expecting a different and better result.

As a leader, how do you get others to embrace the same level of commitment that you have? Sam Walton had the unique ability, as a leader, to get others to buy into his Wal-Mart Way of doing things. His executive team adopted his philosophies when he was still alive, and they have continued to follow Mr. Sam's example to this day. At Wal-Mart, you are either on the team and committed to the goals of the company, or you are not. It's black or white. You can't straddle the commitment line at Wal-Mart; you either have both feet in and you are fully engaged and committed, or you have both feet out and you need to leave the company to pursue your own interests. Half-hearted commitment or having one foot in and one foot out doesn't cut it at the world's largest company.

Sam Walton developed several interesting ways to sort out those who were truly committed from those who were not; for the uncommitted or those who shirked responsibility, there was no place to hide. To be a partner on Sam Walton's team, you had to think like a retail merchant, provide superior customer service, treat people right, and travel out to the stores. Every manager at the home office is required to work a 5½-day work week all year long, including attending the company's famous Saturday morning meetings. That, in itself, takes a tremendous amount of personal commitment. At these meetings, company leaders discuss fresh market intelligence gathered that week from across the world. Regardless of one's job or department, every leader hears the same information and each gets the chance to provide input into the strategies and tactics. Any associate who does not have a point of view on how to improve service to the customer or on other aspects of the operation is clearly disengaged, which is a pretty good indication at Wal-Mart that you aren't committed.

Sam Walton believed in leading by example. I still remember walking past Mr. Sam's office in the final months of his life and seeing him laying flat on his back in a hospital-type bed while continuing to work. There he was taking chemotherapy treatments, with his pen poised and scribbling notes on his legal pad, continuing to the very end to try to think of a better way of doing things. It was shocking to see him continuing to work in his weakened state. I was inspired by the fact that his company, his work, and his associates were that important to him. That image of him lying in that hospital bed in his office working right to the very end is forever burned into my memory. This may seem extreme to some, but that's how committed Sam Walton was to his dreams.

If you want to achieve your full potential, live each and every day with enthusiasm and purpose. Have goals for your career and for your life. The good news is that what you lack in knowledge, skills, and ability can be overcome through sheer determination to succeed. Believe in yourself and believe in your dreams. Remember these inspirational words from Mr. Sam, as you commit to your personal success: "It is not easy when you strive to be the best, but in the long run, it is worth it!"

SHARE SUCCESS with Those Who Have Helped You

Associate profit sharing is the fuel
Sam Walton used to propel
Wal-Mart's rocket to success!

When I worked at Wal-Mart's Home Office, I was sur-
rounded by some of the wealthiest people I had ever
known. I am not talking about the executives or upper level managers here; I'm talking about the hourly paid associates and first-
line supervisors who had dedicated their working careers to
Wal-Mart. It wasn't just home office associates either. I ran into
associates in the stores and distribution centers and even truck
drivers who were fabulously wealthy beyond their wildest dreams.
These are wage earners who were smart enough to buy Wal-
Mart's company stock through payroll deductions and to hold
onto that stock over the years. Through a combination of profit
sharing and the associate stock purchase plan, Wal-Mart's associates became owners of Wal-Mart's company stock. Over the years
the growth of the company and its exceptional performance have
led to eleven 2-for-1 stock splits. The rewards for associates who
dedicated their working life to the company are staggering; many
became rich from those stock splits as they continued to work in
hourly paid positions. Many of the truck drivers and distribution
center and store associates who participated in the profit sharing
and associate stock purchase plans are millionaires, some many
times over. It's the American dream come true!

Sam Walton's second success secret for achieving remarkable
results is *"SHARE SUCCESS with those who have helped you,"*
and it is the most important strategy he implemented back at
the time Wal-Mart first became a public company. Sam Walton's
profit-sharing philosophy was based on his belief that "individuals don't win, teams do" and for Wal-Mart to succeed required
the efforts of everyone on the payroll. Through this single innovation, profit sharing, he transformed his army of associates into
a high-performing team of loyal and motivated business partners.
That loyalty has catapulted Wal-Mart to the top of the *Fortune*

500 list and simultaneously created wealth for Wal-Mart's associates exceeding everyone's expectations.

President Eisenhower said, "Persuasion is the art of getting people to do what you want them to do, and to like it." His point was that before you try to convince someone to do what you want, ask them questions to find out what it is they want. Then, by motivating them to action by showing them how they can get what they want, you can help them achieve their goals, and in turn organizations can achieve their goals. Sam Walton embraced this concept with his profit-sharing program. Since associates had a piece of the action, they wanted to do the things necessary to help Wal-Mart attain its objectives. Mr. Sam was a very smart man who realized that people are Wal-Mart's most important asset. He understood that by treating them as partners and empowering them to serve the customers, he was unleashing a powerful business catalyst called ownership. Sam Walton was ahead of his time. He believed in the benefits of internal customer service, empowerment, and ownership years before those concepts became the program de jour, touted by business consultants around the world.

Sam Walton believed that by sharing profits with all associates you are treating them the way you would treat a partner. By doing so, the normal relationship companies and managers typically have with employees changes. Employees who are treated as partners begin to act like partners in their interactions with customers, suppliers and their own managers. Partners are empowered people, and thus employees begin to feel empowered and take their responsibilities more seriously and enthusiastically. The result, in the case of Wal-Mart, is sales, service, and expense control exceeding the expectations of company leaders. By totally involving his associates in the business, Mr. Sam was successful in instilling pride in his associates, and those good feelings carried over into goal-setting, goal achievement, and then winning at retail. By providing profit sharing to all of his associates and empowering them to do their jobs Mr. Sam received tremendous loyalty from his associates.

You have to remember that profit sharing wasn't commonplace back in 1970. For Mr. Sam to agree to provide such a lucrative benefit to all of his employees indicates his understanding of human psychology. He understood that employees who own company stock have a stake in the success of that company; he figured out the powerful cause-and-effect relationship between offering an incentive to the associates in exchange for increased productivity. Well-stocked shelves, positive customer service, monitoring shoplifting, working safely, and quickly moving customers through the checkout lines all drop big-time dollars to the bottom line. Profit sharing is another example of Sam Walton's willingness to innovate, forcing other companies to imitate. Mr. Sam believed that the creation of the profit-sharing program at Wal-Mart was the single best thing the company had ever done.

I asked one of Wal-Mart's store managers how the company actually used profit sharing to get the associates to act like partners and he said:

> If the associates know what is going on, and if you're being honest with them about your business and what it needs, they will perform. I've seen that time and time again. Whatever your problems are, share them with your associates. A lot of business leaders out there won't share the intimate details about their company. I think Wal-Mart, to my knowledge, is one of the very few companies that will actually take the profit and loss statement and share it with the cashiers and cart-

pushers. If they know what is going on, if they know where your shrinkage issues are and theft issues are, they'll take ownership along with you and help correct the problems. Then, when you are successful, you have to share that with them. That's what Wal-Mart's stakeholder's bonus program is about and the 401k, profit-sharing program is all about. The associates understand that they really are partners here and that creates tremendous ownership.

Helen Walton was influential in convincing Mr. Sam that sharing profits with all of Wal-Mart's associates was a good idea. At first Mr. Sam restricted profit sharing to managers only, but eventually Helen's influence changed his way of thinking and he offered profit sharing to all of his associates. Sam Walton figured out that by giving his associates a piece of the action, by sharing profits with them, he could simultaneously set high standards, keep morale high, and control turnover.

Back in 1970, Sam Walton started providing profit sharing to all of his managers. After Helen's intervention, Mr. Sam implemented a profit-sharing plan for all of the hourly associates the following year. Mr. Sam's profit-sharing design meant taking a percentage of Wal-Mart's profits, putting it in a pool, and disbursing it to company associates some time after the end of the fiscal year. Wal-Mart's profit-sharing program draws people into the process. It drives the value of the company by educating the associates on what they can do on the job to impact the success of the company. Company leaders provide associates with a thorough understanding of their jobs as well as the overall operation of the store or facility where they work. This knowledge empowers associates at all levels to impact the business, thereby increasing their own chances of receiving profit sharing. A profitable operation

increases job security and profit sharing improves every participating associate's standard of living. It's a win-win situation!

The way participation in the plan works is this: every associate
who has worked for the company for at least one year and who
works at least 1,000 hours a year is eligible to have about 6 percent of his or her wages put into a personal profit-sharing plan
account. When they leave the company, they take whatever is in
their plan—in cash or Wal-Mart stock. Profit sharing changed the
way associates felt about working for Wal-Mart from that point
onward. A store manager shared this success story with me to
illustrate the power of profit sharing:

> There are stories of Wal-Mart truck drivers who started out in
> the early days purchasing Wal-Mart stock and who partici-
> pated in profit sharing who retired as millionaires many times
> over. They owned some of the original shares of Wal-Mart
> stock. The performance of the stock is not the same today, but
> the opportunities within the company definitely are. There are
> different programs in place. Now as a store manager you have
> a bonus program, you still have a stock purchase plan that
> offers good potential, and you also have a 401k program that
> has partial matching. I think from a benefits standpoint Wal-
> Mart is still as good an opportunity as it ever was.

Sam Walton always believed the associates were the key to
growing the business and their relationship with the company had
to be a partnership. Creating that partnership required a good
flow of communication and an ongoing exchange of ideas. It also
demanded that everyone constructively critique every area of the
operation and even the way managers and associates behaved. That
partnership, coupled with treating the customers right, would prove
to be the catalyst Mr. Sam used to grow the company. He knew it

was his associate partners in the day-in and day-out contact with the customers who would ultimately determine the success or failure of his vision for the company. By sharing profits, he'd have happy employees; happy employees create a positive shopping experience for the customers and that means more sales at the registers. By giving his associates a stake in the company through profit sharing, Mr. Sam figured out he could instill the same feeling of ownership in all of the associates that he felt personally by providing everyone with the incentive to drive sales, serve customers, and control expenses. In the early days company profit sharing engendered powerful loyalty to both Sam Walton and his company from all of his associates. Over the years associate loyalty has proven to be one of the great catalysts of Wal-Mart's unprecedented growth domestically and internationally. It is that loyalty that has kept the company nonunion and driven company sales to almost $300 billion annually.

Back in Wal-Mart's "go-go" years, in the 1970s and 1980s, when the stock split nine times, Mr. Sam believed that it was the profit-sharing program that fueled the success of the company. In his autobiography he said, "Profit sharing has pretty much been the carrot that's kept Wal-Mart moving forward." There is little doubt the Wal-Mart rural retailing concept was the right idea at the right time. By going public in 1970, Sam Walton had the necessary infusion of cash to grow the company but it was the associates who stoked the fires. Some would argue that motivating rich people to work is harder than motivating wage earners, but not at Wal-Mart. With the roll-out of the profit-sharing program, Mr. Sam uncovered the hidden potential in his workforce. His team of associates became his true business partners, as interested as he was in making the company successful. Profit sharing at

Wal-Mart was like pouring gasoline on a burning ember; it fueled the explosive growth of the company, and that growth continues to this day.

I saw the power of profit sharing firsthand. Some of the people working around me at the Wal-Mart home office had been through many stock splits. It seemed like everyone purchased Wal-Mart stock through payroll deduction in the company's Associate Stock Purchase Program. Many of the long-term associates at Wal-Mart and Sam's Club, management and hourly, own company stock valued in the mid- to high-six-figure range and some are into seven figures. It's interesting to note that in the world of instant "spoiled brat" millionaires resulting from all of these IPOs (initial public offerings of stock) in recent years, you'll never meet a friendlier, less pretentious, and harder working group of wealthy folks than you'll find at Wal-Mart and Sam's Club.

The great secret to Wal-Mart's profit-sharing program is its ability to provide incentive and to motivate people to achieve Mr. Sam's lofty goals. In an article entitled "Sam's Dream," Washington Post reporter Wells Tower talks about Wal-Mart's unique employees:

> Wal-Mart's "associates" are, by and large, people who don't have extensive employment options arrayed before them: women returning to the workforce after long stints of stay-at-home motherhood; teenagers trying out paid labor for the first time; people transitioning off of welfare; older folks, who can't get by on Social Security alone. Many people here have worked other low-wage jobs, but they come to Wal-Mart because, above the din of tolling cash registers, they hear that this is a different sort of company, one that cares for its employees as much as its bottom line. They speak ardently

about Sam Walton's partnership with associates, and of the limitless future Wal-Mart represents. ("You can make your own future here," an associate declared. "Look above the sky, beyond the clouds. Let your light shine for others to see!") Associates talk earnestly about cashiers who have retired with millions in their retirement accounts (to which the company contributes Wal-Mart stock), about how here a high school diploma is all one needs to ascend to upper management and command the kind of salary other companies pay only to pedigreed MBAs.*

We know Wal-Mart's profit sharing has made lots of its associates financially secure, but what does the company get in return? First and foremost the company is able to attract and retain the best quality associates available in the local market. Once those associates are onboard they have a tendency to stay. The combination of profit sharing and being treated like a partner provides a powerful incentive for associates to stay. Secondarily, it provides a reason to get excited and have fun at work every day. Happy associates mean happy customers. Mr. Sam realized that once associates got their first profit-sharing statement, they understood that feeling of ownership on a personal level and the importance of being a true business partner. It is that feeling that drives them in the future to do what they can to positively impact the things within their control in the stores, distribution center, fleet, specialty divisions, and home office.

---

*From the washingtonpost.com article called, "Sam's Dream" by Wells Tower, Sunday, October 6, 2002; Page W06. *http://www.washingtonpost.com/ac2/wp-dyn?pagename=article&node=&contentId=A38613-2002Oct3&notFound=true.*

Company managers teach willing associates to dramatically improve shelf restocking, enhance the quality of service, and reduce costs, which all have a direct impact on year-end profit sharing. The associates willingly participate in goal-setting processes so they understand what is important to focus upon to improve company profitability. The company's managers share confidential company financial information with their associate partners so they understand exactly how the company is doing every month of the year. All of these steps ultimately lead to the creation of an "employee owner" mentality. Associates who feel like owners will go to extraordinary lengths to improve every aspect of the operation. Mr. Sam knew that by setting clear goals, providing frequent feedback, creating team-based incentives, and setting goals that required everyone to exert extra effort that company profitability targets would be hit and the company would prosper.

All of Wal-Mart associates become eligible to share in the company's profits after one year of employment and 1,000 hours of service have been completed. Profit sharing is funded 100 percent by Wal-Mart, and the funds are primarily invested in Wal-Mart stock. Both full-time and part-time associates are eligible to share in the profits. Wal-Mart also offers hourly and management associates an incentive/bonus plan based on company performance. The bonus they are eligible to receive is a percentage of their wage as additional income based on performance. Hourly and full-time associates also may receive a holiday bonus that is based on length of service with the company. There are also many other incentives that are offered on an individual basis.

The beauty of profit sharing from Mr. Sam's perspective was that there was no downside. Rewards were clearly tied to organizational performance. If the company hit its goals, the associates benefited;

if organizational goals aren't met, profit sharing doesn't get paid. All of the potential for Sam Walton and Wal-Mart was upside potential. Once those first profit-sharing statements were delivered to associates, everybody understood "what's in it for me!" From that point onward entrepreneurial-minded associates were willing to do whatever it took to make the business as successful as it could be. One of Wal-Mart's store managers told me, "Mr. Sam wasn't the kind of person who was going to give anybody anything—they had to earn it. He thought everybody ought to participate in the success of the operation and by doing so influence their own future. Profit sharing was a also way to keep people with the company because his associates had something nobody else in the industry was offering. It was like you owned part of that company."

If you think about it, there is no one who takes their ownership responsibilities more seriously than a small business owner who is an independent entrepreneur or what is termed a sole proprietor. There truly is no one more motivated and involved in the world of business. Entrepreneurs will do whatever it takes to make their business successful, and long hours are just one part of their labor of love. Twelve- to fourteen-hour work days, seven days a week are the norm. Multitasking is a way of life and business owners are problem solving machines. They don't steal, waste company resources, or complain about having to work long hours. Work–life balance is a foreign concept to them. They are willing to sacrifice it all in order to succeed. If taking time away from the family is required, so be it. As far as Sam Walton was concerned, these entrepreneurial types had everything he saw in himself. They were innovative, problem solvers who were willing to go the distance. Mr. Sam liked to hire entrepreneurial-minded people in his stores. With them on the team, Wal-Mart was poised to be a real contender. These were his perfect partners!

Mr. Sam liked people who exhibited entrepreneurial commitment, spirit and passion. The quotation that follows is called "The Entrepreneur," and these words capture the way he lived his life and ran his business and provides competitive insights into Sam Walton the business leader:

> I do not choose to be a common man. It is my right to be uncommon. I seek opportunity...not security. I do not wish to be a kept citizen, humbled and dulled by having the state look after me. I want to take the calculated risk; to dream and to build, to fail and to succeed. I refuse to barter incentive for a dole. I prefer the challenges of life to the guaranteed existence; the thrill of fulfillment to the stale calm of utopia. I will not trade freedom for beneficence, nor my dignity, for a handout. I will never cower before any master nor bend to any threat. It is my heritage to stand erect, proud and unafraid; to think and act for myself; enjoy the benefits of my creations and to face the world boldly and say, this, with God's help, I have done. And this is what it means to be an entrepreneur.
>
> —Anonymous

The kinds of personal attributes exhibited by Sam Walton are the same attributes it takes to be a successful entrepreneur or a success in any business. Here's a list which describes Sam Walton's own leadership style: high energy, determination, perseverance, passion, commitment, self-confidence, goal orientation, action orientation, can-do attitude, problem solver, innovator, continuous learner, competitive with a need to achieve, good listener, inspirational leader, people orientation, success celebrator, self-starter, self-reliance, risk taker, servant leader, and team oriented and he was a fact finder, not a fault finder. Mr. Sam seemed to like the people around him to share many of those same leadership characteristics.

Another reason Mr. Sam liked entrepreneurs was because of their entrepreneurial spirit, drive, and proven track record of running their own businesses. Many of them were doing just that when he first met them. Imagine having Sam Walton walk in the front door of your business observing whether or not you run a good operation. That's what Mr. Sam would do. Many of his early managers had owned their own businesses so they were already entrepreneurial-minded, which made their transition into Wal-Mart easier. Once these former business owners and entrepreneurs transitioned into Wal-Mart, Mr. Sam referred to them as "intrapreneurs."

Instilling an entrepreneurial feeling of ownership was pivotal to Mr. Sam's ability to create a true business partnership with those early managers and associates. An intrapreneur is defined as an entrepreneur who works within a corporation. Intrapreneurial ownership later became the foundation upon which Wal-Mart's profit-sharing program was based. Mr. Sam realized true owners were totally motivated and involved in every aspect of the business because they had a financial stake. They owned the business and reaped the fruits of their labor if it made money. They would also take it on the chin if the company lost money.

At Wal-Mart, intrapreneurial leadership isn't restricted to management types; all associates are encouraged to act like business owners. Mr. Sam expected leaders to live up to high standards; he always said, "High expectations are the key to everything." So to be a true intrapreneurial leader, according to Mr. Sam, you would have to be willing to do any job required regardless of your job description. The true intrapreneurial leader shares credit for successes with everyone on the team. He used to say, "It's amazing what a group of people can accomplish if no one worries about who is going to get the credit." He believed everyone should try new ways of doing things and take risks. Because he valued thrift, it was important for effective company leaders to get things done creatively, with the resources at hand, without the need to spend company money. Mr. Sam's view of an effective intrapreneur was someone who stayed focused on company goals and did what was necessary to achieve those goals as if they owned the company.

When it came to hiring hourly associates, Mr. Sam figured out that, on average, people actually relish the idea of being given responsibility; they also like to be held accountable because it makes them feel important. Using the same approach he had used to hire managers, Mr. Sam looked for employees who were willing to go the extra yard for his customers. He had a unique ability to size people up quickly. I think that was because of his active listening skills and his powers of observation. In any case, it didn't take him long to get to know what made someone tick. Once he found associates who were willing to take ownership, he'd get them to refer their friends and relatives who shared those same values.

Staffing was and still remains one of the biggest challenges Wal-Mart's leaders face. Mr. Sam knew he had to find people to work across the organization who were innovative and creative, upbeat and positive, generalists versus specialists as well as hard-working and fun-loving. When he hired people for his stores, he hired for attitude; he was not overly concerned with prior job experience. It was that belief that created unbelievable opportunities for average people at Wal-Mart. He created a symbiotic relationship where associates could achieve their personal goals while they worked hard to help him achieve his corporate Wal-Mart objectives. He encouraged the philosophy that everyone in Wal-Mart can be as successful as they choose to be if they are entrepreneurial-minded and if they are willing to work together as a member of the team.

Unless an associate really doesn't care (a bad hire), ownership brings an immediate sense of belonging and importance at Wal-

Mart. Everybody wants to be somebody, and Wal-Mart gives every associate the chance to achieve his or her personal goals. The foundation skills learned as an hourly associate at Wal-Mart are so important to the success of the organization that promotion from within is the norm. If you want to understand the key to Wal-Mart's success, you need look no further than the empowered associates who take their company ownership very seriously. Mr. Sam would tell you that the driving force behind Wal-Mart's monumental success is the associate profit sharing that has served as the primary fuel which Sam Walton used to propel Wal-Mart's rocket to success.

So how does Wal-Mart take the unbridled enthusiasm of over a million associates in all those stores and channel all of that energy to achieve company goals? They do it with what is called a "stakeholder's bonus" (today referred to as "My $hare") in every store tied to specific and measurable criteria. All store associates are eligible to participate in the bonus plan. It's one of the reasons that Wal-Mart has been able to run its operations nonunion across the United States. I got one of Wal-Mart's former managers to share insights on the program:

> It's called a stakeholder's bonus not a stockholder's bonus! (Stakeholder's bonus is Wal-Mart's term for a store-level profit-sharing program.) The stores monitor it monthly and we make a big deal out of it. We have a big chart in the hallway where the associates clock in and clock out so everyone is able to see it. Every month when we get the store profit-and-loss statement we update the numbers and basically it gives the associates the ability to monitor the numbers. It breaks down your sales, your margin, how much of that is profit, what has to come out of that profit, and then down at the bottom whatever the dollar amount that is actually profit year to date, a percentage of which goes into the stakeholder's plan for your store. At the end of the year, whatever is in that stakeholder's plan gets divided up among the hourly associates and

assistant managers in the store. Full-time associates get a full share and part-timers get a half share, and you have to be on the payroll for 6 months and a day during the fiscal year. In a good year, the full-time associates could receive a stakeholder's bonus check of $1000 each and part time associates could receive $500. The stakeholder's bonus plan was put in place to encourage associates to take ownership in their store because contrary to popular opinion, Wal-Mart isn't this huge company based out of Bentonville, Arkansas. It's really 6,700 individual stores. We truly run each store as ours and the associates of that store have a vested interest to make that store as profitable, as customer friendly, in-stock and as clean as you can possibly get it because we're all going to benefit from that.

The good news is that when Wal-Mart's tough goals are met the associates share in the rewards. The bad news is that not every associate on the team performs at an acceptable level. Slackers aren't tolerated. In fact, Wal-Mart's leaders aren't shy about aggressively confronting those associates who aren't pulling their share of the load. In addition, the peer pressure from other associates who feel their bonus is being threatened is enough to snap nonperforming team members back to an acceptable performance level or it drives them out of the company. This combination of rewarding performance and dealing with nonperformance is the catalyst driving the Wal-Mart performance machine. It's Sam Walton's version of the carrot and the stick; company leaders have turned profit sharing into a competitive advantage. Imagine all of those associates chomping at the bit to improve customer service and reduce costs in order to impact their own profit sharing. Wal-Mart's profit-sharing formula is one part goal setting, one part empowerment of individuals, one part team synergy, and one part ongoing management communication of key metrics, which yields goal achievement, profit sharing, and undying loyalty from its associates. It's actually a pretty straightforward win-win process that allowed Sam Walton to use the concept of associate partnership as a way to capture the hearts and minds of Wal-Mart's people.

Profit sharing is not a "something for nothing" proposition, however. At Wal-Mart I was taught to confront nonperforming associates and not to accept less than acceptable performance. One of the interesting reasons I was told to do so is because managers need to give the associates who are doing a good job a reason to continue performing well. The manager who knowingly allows nonperformers to continue working at an unacceptable level is a manager whose own performance will soon be called into question at Wal-Mart. For this reason, company managers aren't shy about taking on associate performance problems; it is expected. Using a four-step coaching and counseling process, managers give nonperforming associates an opportunity to improve performance, using performance coaching. The goal of dealing with associate performance problems is to correct the problem, not to terminate the associate. Ninety percent of those who have performance issues who go through performance coaching are able to turn their performance around and stay with the company.

Employees in your organization and the associates at Wal-Mart aren't stupid. They know when one of his or her fellow employees isn't doing their fair share of the work. When a manager or supervisor deals with nonperformers, word gets around without management saying a word. Everybody finds out and typically it is the nonperforming employee who tells everyone around them that they were disciplined. Organizationally, that is actually a good thing because your good performers expect you to deal with those who aren't performing. It is not uncommon for morale and workgroup performance to actually rise following a performance coaching incident. Employees expect supervisors to take on performance problems, and they respect the supervisor who will do so. On the flip side, the supervisor who won't hold people accountable is contributing to lower morale and job performance in his or her own workgroup. Said another way, that supervisor has become part of the problem. The team at Wal-Mart is only as strong as its weakest link, and to achieve profit sharing is an all-or-none proposition. The weak links can be the difference between the achievement of a store's profit-sharing goals and missing those goals. Failing to achieve profit sharing because of a few bad apples can have a devastating affect on morale overall.

In order to make the profit-sharing program successful, Wal-Mart's managers have to clearly communicate company expectations to the associates. Once the associates know their role and what the target is, it is now up to the company's managers to provide feedback on company performance. Without giving regular updates to employees a profit-sharing program loses visibility. Out of sight is out of mind, and for Wal-Mart's program to succeed requires the total support of everyone on the team. No profit-sharing program will work if company leaders and managers don't work at it constantly. It's particularly important to help new associates understand what's in it for them if they work to achieve the goals of the company. So how does Wal-Mart keep the idea of profit sharing in the front of everyone's mind? Wal-Mart leaders talk about it all year long.

At daily "stand-up" meetings company managers review current sales, payroll budgets, and shrinkage (theft numbers). You may be thinking daily meetings are overkill. In actuality, I have never heard an organization accused of providing too much information to employees. On the contrary, many would be accused of not providing enough. Some might be accused of not providing any. Information is power at Wal-Mart. Sam Walton believed that for profit sharing to work you have to communicate to keep it out in front of everybody at all times. The associates have to understand how the their store or distribution center is performing relative to plan if management expects those associates to make the necessary adjustments to impact the business, today. By communicating the profit-sharing message overtly or subliminally, each and every day, the associates are focused on achieving company goals with the realization that if those goals are attained, rewards will follow.

If there was one thing Mr. Sam would say to make the business case for profit sharing, it's in his belief that "If you will take care of your people, it is your people who will take care of your customers and the business will take care of itself." Sam Walton figured out that people are motivated for their own reasons, not someone else's; it's the concept called "WIIFM," *What's In It for Me*! His ideas for sharing profits with associates were clearly ahead of their time, serving as another example of Mr. Sam's ability to think outside the box. The loyalty of his associates and the ownership they take of the business are an important part of his success story. Remember what Sam Walton always used to tell the associates: "If someone asks you 'who owns Wal-Mart?' look them straight in the eye and tell them YOU do!"

MOTIVATE Yourself and Others to Achieve Your Dreams

Mr. Sam hired ordinary people off the
farms around Bentonville and
by doing so provided many of them
with opportunities beyond
their wildest dreams.

One of the great motivational stories about Sam Walton I personally experienced came out of Wal-Mart's famous shareholders' meetings. Unlike any other in the world, Mr. Sam's meeting was an event to celebrate the success of the company and the associates and a time to appreciate those who had enough confidence in Sam Walton to invest in his company. Thousands of people would show up in northwest Arkansas for the annual extravaganza held at the Benton County Fairgrounds in the early days and in later years up to 14,000 at the University of Arkansas basketball pavilion. Almost every other shareholder's meeting at corporations across America is attended by very few stockholders. Even recent examples of meetings, come to mind, that were well attended, were a result of hostile stockholders interested in changing that company's management.

Mr. Sam's meeting was one part business, one part inspiration, and one part circus! He was known to stand at one of the entrances to meet, greet, and shake hands with attendees as they arrived. Sam Walton ran the show like he was running a three-ring circus. His meetings were fun, inspirational, and full of surprises. Often he had to be reminded by his executive team to cover business-related topics in order to officially meet the legal requirements of an annual shareholders' meeting. Mr. Sam was the best motivational leader of a major corporation I have ever seen. He had a unique talent for getting everyone around him as excited about his business as he was. Mr. Sam believed that if you act enthusiastic, you'll be enthusiastic and those around you will become energized.

"MOTIVATE yourself and others to achieve your dreams" is Mr. Sam's third success secret for achieving remarkable results. Rule number 3 addresses the importance of having a motivated team of managers and associates to achieving the goals at any organization. Sam Walton realized money in and of itself doesn't

motivate people; people motivate people. Managers have a role in creating a positive environment within which people can flourish; however, true motivation comes from within the individual associate. He believed in setting aggressive goals and challenging his associates to achieve them. Rarely did they disappoint him.

Mark Twain once said, "Keep away from people who try to belittle your ambitions. Small people always do that, but the really great ones make you feel that you too, can become great." That's exactly the way Sam Walton made the people around him feel. Mr. Sam had a unique talent for seeing in people the potential to achieve great things and he provided them with opportunities to realize that potential. He implored his leadership team to "believe in people more than they believe in themselves." He knew that his associates had the ability to accomplish whatever he asked them to do. On their own, associates sometimes lack the confidence or belief in their own ability. Sam Walton knew that people use just a fraction of their potential and if he took the time to nurture and train them, that potential would come pouring out.

To avoid stagnation, he believed in moving people cross-functionally into jobs for which they had no previous training. He also believed in creating an ever-changing and unpredictable work environment in order to break the potential monotony sometimes associated with the retail store environment. His never-ending goal was to have the most positive employees in retail who were motivated to exceed his customers' expectations.

I remember attending the Saturday morning meeting held every week of the year at the Bentonville home office. Mr. Sam ran these meetings and he was known for coming up with fun and interesting distractions to entertain those in attendance; he always made it a surprise, and part of the fun was in not knowing what he'd come up with next. One Saturday he brought his hunting dogs to the headquarters and set them loose to run the halls. Another Saturday he would have a country western singer or a Hollywood celebrity attend the meeting. They would come to promote an album or their latest movie, and Mr. Sam would introduce them to everyone in attendance. By breaking up the routine and having fun, Sam Walton took the edge off the ever-present stress associated with running the world's largest and most successful company.

Sam Walton believed that goal setting was a critical component to the success of Wal-Mart and Sam's Club. Company leaders even created the acronym *HEATKTE* which stands for *high expectations are the key to everything*. The idea behind HEATKTE was the creation of a high-performance self-fulfilling prophecy. Sam's Club leaders believed so strongly in the concept of HEATKTE that they even created a company chant that included a ritualistic song and a dance that was enthusiastically acted out at gatherings with associates to reinforce company standards and expectations. HEATKTE was quite literally a company rallying cry for higher levels of achievement.

As I talk about results through people at Wal-Mart, remember the words of the HEATKTE acronym because *high expectations ARE the key to everything* at your organization as well. If you supervise employees, there are times you actually have to believe in people more than they believe in themselves, just as Sam Walton did. By believing in them, Mr. Sam instilled confidence in average people who may or may not have known they had the ability to perform at above-average levels. Once Mr. Sam's associates figured out that he had confidence in them, they had the resolve to achieve even the highest standards.

The same lesson holds true for you and the people in your organization. If your team knows you have faith in their abilities, you can stand back and witness the seemingly impossible become reality. You'll soon find you can set the performance bar higher than you ever imagined you could, and you keep raising it as people prove to you they can achieve their goals, over and over again. You'll find your employees are more than equal to the challenge. What was once a stretch goal becomes, over a period of time, normal and average employee behavior. Mr. Sam was the master of creating challenges and achieving results through the creation of his own version of a self-fulfilling prophecy. His unwavering belief in people and his sincere encouragement of their efforts have almost always led to awe-inspiring results.

Why was Sam Walton able to make this happen? At times I think it had as much to do with the fact that they didn't want to let *him* down as it did with their own internal drive. In other words, they achieved out of love and respect for him as a leader, and because they knew he wanted them to achieve, they didn't want to let him down. This leadership motivation technique is built around the idea that if a supervisor sincerely cares about the employees as people, the employees will then care about the needs of the business. Similarly, employees don't care how much their supervisor knows until they know how much that individual cares about them. Mr. Sam was a master motivator of people. He realized the job of a supervisor is to achieve company business goals through the efforts and results of a team of people. His form of employee motivation has become culturally engrained at Wal-Mart and continues to be reinforced through his belief that executives, managers, and supervisors need to be "servant leaders."

Sam Walton's vision for Wal-Mart was to create a fast-growing, customer-focused company known for being a "fast adapter"; a company with a deep understanding of customer wants and needs that is able to change directions quickly to meet those needs. In order to achieve his vision, he understood the importance of having motivated associates who would adapt to the Wal-Mart way. He believed in promotion from within and the associates had walking, talking examples all around them of managers who had been rewarded for their efforts with bigger jobs and more responsibility. Opportunity is disguised as hard work at Wal-Mart and for those who are smart enough to recognize that fact, the career opportunities are endless.

Interestingly, when the U.S. Department of Labor did a study on what motivates people at work, they found managers and employees selected the same 9 factors in their top 10 motivators list when given the same 23 factors to choose from. Here are the two lists:

Salaried Management
Interesting work
Opportunities to develop special abilities
Enough information
Enough authority
Enough help and equipment
Friendly and helpful co-workers
Opportunity to see the results of work
Competent supervision
Responsibilities clearly defined
Good pay

Hourly Paid Workers
Good pay
Enough help and equipment
Job security
Enough information
Interesting work
Friendly and helpful co-workers

Responsibilities clearly defined
Opportunity to see results of work
Enough authority
Competent supervision

There are only two uniquely selected items on the two lists. The first is "opportunities to develop special abilities" on the salaried management list and the second is "job security" on the hourly paid workers list. All of the rest of the job factors selected are the same. The only other differences in the two lists of motivators are the order of importance attributed to the individual items by each group. What this says is what Sam Walton already knew from experience: that all people are motivated by very similar goals and aspirations in life and in their work. By figuring this out, Mr. Sam was able to motivate his entire team with the same messages going out to managers and associates. In other words, he treated all of his associates as partners, each associate equally as important as any associate. That message has been well received over the years by his associates and managers, and the success of the company is its best indicator.

Like Mr. Sam, Wal-Mart's associates have a distinct set of characteristics that set them apart. Here is list of culturally engrained motivational attributes, planted firmly in the culture by Mr. Sam himself, which capture the characteristics of Wal-Mart's managers and associates and the Wal-Mart way:

- Passion for the bottom line
- Customer-centered relationships
- Bias for results
- Innovation
- Integrity/honesty/trust

- Risk taking
- Passion for quality
- People make the difference
- Everyone's a leader

Allow me to review for you each of these motivational attributes.

Passion for the bottom line. Wal-Mart's managers and associates team up to attack the achievement of the aggressive goals of the company. With store-based incentives available and company profit-sharing plans everyone has a vested interest in impacting the bottom line. Associates are encouraged to be leaders and everyone is expected to compete aggressively with a will to win.

Customer-centered relationships. It's a merchandise-driven business and Mr. Sam expected everyone to think like a merchant. "Drop everything for the customer, the 10-foot rule, the sundown rule, VPI, and internal customer service" are all cultural standards at Wal-Mart. Each of these programs will be reviewed in detail in the chapter devoted to rule 8. Sam Walton appreciated the efforts of all of the associates in serving the customers and he often said the associates closest to the customers were the most important people in the company. Without those customers going through the registers, everybody would be out of a job.

Bias for results. Once Wal-Mart establishes goals, the company stays committed to them. Retailers like Wal-Mart are notorious for their orientation toward action. Wal-Mart's army of ordinary people is focused to achieve extraordinary results. Everyone is expected to have a strong sense of urgency and have a determination to get things done, NOW!

Innovation. Most of the best ideas have come from the bottom up, not from the top down like they do in so many organizations. Mr. Sam always believed the people closest to the customer in one of his stores or the people closest to the work in a distribution center have the most creative solutions to business-related problems. He called it a "grass roots philosophy." If you're smart enough to ask them, they'll provide better ideas than their managers would come up with, and they'll do it quickly!

Integrity/honesty/trust. The culture at Wal-Mart is based on trust. So are the relationships with suppliers and vendors. If the associates at Wal-Mart say they are going to do something, they do it. Sam Walton had zero tolerance for people who lacked integrity; in fact, dishonesty was the quickest way for a supplier to get kicked out of his stores or for an associate to lose his or her job. The unique character of the associates of Wal-Mart starts with a solid foundation of honesty and integrity.

Risk taking. The associates at Wal-Mart are encouraged to try new ways of doing things, which on occasion will lead to some inevitable failures. The company's leaders have a high tolerance for taking calculated risks. If an idea works, it is communicated across the chain of stores; if it fails, they learn from it and are careful not to make the same mistake twice. The associates have a low resistance to change and for that reason are willing to try almost anything; company managers have the same attitude. Mr. Sam believed that Wal-Mart would never be as good as it could be without a willingness on the part of leaders and associates to try new and different ways of doing things and by doing so to learn to tolerate failure on occasion.

Passion for quality. Mr. Sam was a continuous learner and he believed in continuous improvement long before the ideas of quality gurus like Juran, Crosby, and Deming were widely followed in the United States. He inspired a culture full of curious people who, like him, were always trying to figure out a better way. Total quality management techniques like process flow charting are taught to hourly paid employees, who use them to evaluate complex processes in order to squeeze out cost savings and reduce the time required to complete tasks. For years, Mr. Sam benchmarked his practices against Malcolm Baldrige Award–winning manufacturing companies who supplied products to his stores. Companies like General Electric and Procter & Gamble are what Mr. Sam called *vendor partners* that have helped Wal-Mart improve everything from product distribution to inventory technology. In reverse, those companies have also learned just as many innovative ideas from the world's largest retailer.

People make the difference. Sam Walton would describe his associates as a diverse collection of mostly average people. When asked how Wal-Mart achieved such incredible success, he would boil it all down to the most important reason: the associates. He believed that competitors who visit the stores can copy the products and merchandising techniques, but the one thing they can't duplicate is the culture of the company and its interested, dedicated, and loyal people.

Everyone's a leader. All of Wal-Mart associates are encouraged to be leaders. In the Wal-Mart culture, a leader is defined as a person who sets examples and is looked up to for his or her actions. This means that anyone is capable of being a leader and that it is not just limited to those holding a management job title. At Wal-Mart, leadership is all based on the simple principle of focusing on making the customer number 1. The way the company turns this concept into reality is through empowerment. Mr. Sam believed in pushing responsibility and authority for decision making as far down the organization as possible. Often that means giving nonmanagement associates "on the spot" decision-making authority in their dealings with customers. This simple concept has increased the number of customer service leaders or decision makers to include Mr. Sam's entire army of associates.

Company managers are also focused on serving the customers. Managers have a specific set of core leadership competencies that Mr. Sam was instrumental in identifying: communication, developing others, motivating others, customer focus listening, continuous improvement, sense of urgency, team development, organization/ planning, expectations/accountability, and resolving problems. I review how Mr. Sam communicated these key leadership competencies in detail in the chapter devoted to rule 4. The job of Wal-Mart's managers is to get things done with and through the efforts of employees. To do this, managers need to create an environment within which associates are motivated to do a good job.

"Hire the best, provide the best training, and be the best place to work" was Sam Walton's cultural mantra at Wal-Mart. He believed in finding and hiring the best available talent, developing their knowledge and skills, and creating an environment within which his associates were proud to work. Don Soderquist, Wal-Mart's former COO, describes the importance of the company's culture to the success of the company: "In my judgment, the culture of Wal-Mart is what made us different. Yes, certainly you have to make the right decisions, you have to have a good business plan, you have to have a profit model that works, and you have to have strong leadership and all the rest. But what made us different and enabled us to accomplish what every other retailer had the ability to accomplish were our values, our core values on which we operated the company, and the values which were intertwined and became a part of our culture."

Sam Walton's founding values for Wal-Mart are respect for the individual, service to the customers, and striving for excellence. The company translates those values as follows:

- Exceeding customer expectations
- Quality in every process
- Professionalism and ethical behavior
- Integrity and honesty in all dealings
- Competitiveness, can-do attitude, and a will to win
- Growth and development of associates
- Continuous productivity improvement
- Continuous learning
- Growing profits for shareholders

These values are the foundation upon which the Wal-Mart way of doing business was built. The same beliefs are as true today as they were over 40 years ago when Sam Walton started the company. Those beliefs are translated into action by company leaders who are hired with the expectation that they deal with others with integrity and honesty, have a strong work ethic, are passionate about their jobs, and are culturally sensitive. The people skills the company most values in its leaders are good communication, developing others, customer focus, strong listening skills, and the ability to motivate others. Here are some questions that will help you understand Wal-Mart's cultural expectations and help you evaluate how motivated you are as an individual:

- Do you have a can-do attitude?
- Do you have strong active listening skills?
- Are you good at managing conflict?
- Are you comfortable taking risks and making mistakes?
- Are you comfortable if others take risks and make mistakes?
- Are you reactive or proactive in your approach to business problems?
- Are you a team builder?
- Do you work well with a diverse workforce and are you culturally sensitive?
- Do you like being a team member yourself?
- Are you willing to give credit to the team for accomplishments and suppress your own need for individual recognition?
- Do you have a high tolerance for stress?
- Are you results driven and solutions oriented?
- Do you have a strong work ethic?
- Are you passionate about what you do?
- Are you a creative thinker?
- Do you like working with and nurturing people?
- Are you an excellent communicator?
- Do you have a strong desire to succeed?

If you answered "YES" to these questions, you have what it takes to be successful at Wal-Mart or in what ever you choose to do.

When you have such a gigantic organization, the motivation level of your people can be an advantage or it can be a disadvantage. At Wal-Mart it is a competitive advantage because of the belief by company leaders that the associates are the key to the success of the company. That belief is the driving force within the culture that creates a self-fulfilling prophecy. It is that belief that motivates a team of average people to believe in themselves, to perform beyond their own expectations, and to achieve at the highest levels. Wal-Mart's culture and its motivated staff give it a competitive advantage in the marketplace.

Motivated employees who feel good about themselves and who are having fun at what they do are better able to project that enthusiasm to others. To provide great customer service requires everyone to have a high degree of personal motivation. In terms of Maslow's hierarchy of needs, providing enthusiastic customer service is a self-actualized behavior. To reach the self-actualized level, so employees can even begin to think about providing knock-your-socks-off service, employees have to have their own needs met first. Once their personal emotional needs are fulfilled, they are then in a position to begin worrying about meeting the emotional needs of others. I have always believed Mr. Sam was a student of human behavior and a bit of a behavioral psychologist. He understood what demotivates people and more importantly what gets them really motivated. Highly motivated employees with good attitudes breed more of the same in the employees and customers around them. Unfortunately, poor attitudes or lack of motivation has a similar impact on others. The bottom line is the bottom line: Enthusiastic people providing great customer service equal company profits.

One of Wal-Mart's former store managers shared this insight with me about Sam Walton's treatment of the associates:

> Mr. Sam had a lot of his success because of the way he was able to treat the people around him and that he was able to make every single associate in that store that he met with feel like he was their friend as well as their boss. He didn't just do it with lip service; he did a lot of things for the associates. He tried to make things better. In fact I think back in the late 80s and early 90s, when they were in the smaller towns, in the middle part of the country, that was the job to have. You had

benefits back then that were comparable with everything else. You had a steady job and you knew Wal-Mart was going to be there. You were working for a man who you knew appreciated you.

Sam Walton realized the impact of positive motivation techniques on the performance of individuals and workgroups. He called the employees "associates" as a sign of respect for the importance of their role in serving customers and keeping Wal-Mart's industry-leading cost structure at the lowest possible levels. True business partners take ownership of the business. Treating employees as partners has resulted in the associates assuming personal ownership for having products in stock, providing terrific service, and controlling costs. Here's a great quote from Sam Walton that captures his beliefs:

> Most managers lead by fear and intimidation. They think that being tough is being a leader. Nothing is further from the truth. Good leaders add the human factor to all aspects of their business. If you manage through fear, your people will be nervous around you. After a while, they won't approach you with a problem, so the problem gets worse. They will be afraid to be creative or express a new idea. They don't feel like they can take a chance because they won't want to risk your disapproval. When this happens, the people suffer, and the business suffers, too. In Wal-Mart, we must treat our people with genuine respect and courtesy. Build strong relationships with your people. Help your associates grow and be all they can be. Show that you really care. You must become a master at communicating with them all aspects of your business and their place in it. The best way you can let them know how much you value their contributions is to show them and tell them, one-on-one. Get to know your people, their families, their problems, their hopes and ambitions. Appreciate and praise them as individuals. Show your concern daily. We are all just

people with varying strengths and weaknesses. So true commitment, plus a generous portion of understanding and communication, will help us win. Leaders must always put their people before themselves. If you do that, your business will take care of itself.*

Mr. Sam figured out so many ways to motivate people. One way was to treat them the way he himself wanted to be treated. He learned a lesson from Dale Carnegie, who said that a person's name is to that person the sweetest sound in any language. For this reason, Mr. Sam established the use of name badges for all of his associates so that everyone acknowledged one another by name. Even he wore a name badge that simply said "Sam." Mr. Sam used some simple techniques for motivating people: smiling, listening, using people's names, and looking people in the eye. Here's a description of how Sam Walton felt about the importance of each to good human relations:

- *Smiling* may seem like a simple idea, but it is truly amazing how many people don't do it. They walk around serious all the time and by doing so put people off around them. Mr. Sam always seemed to have a smile on his face, and he created a feeling of openness and trust by not appearing to be too serious. He believed that by being friendly and smiling you become more approachable in customer relations, family relations, and associate relations. When you smile, it shows you are comfortable with yourself and that you are happy to be with the people around you. You can't be taking

---

*Sam Walton quoted by David Hatch, on the Franklin Covey website *http://www.franklincovey.com/ez/library/samw.html*.

yourself too seriously when you are smiling, and it's impossible to be crabby with a big smile on your face!

- *Listening* is one of the things I remember most about Sam Walton; he had tremendous active listening skills. He gave you the feeling when you talked with him that you were the most important person in the world to him at that moment. Instead of listening to what is being said *to them,* many people are already thinking about what *they* are going to say. Sam Walton once said, "When you are listening to somebody, completely, attentively, then you are listening not only to the words, but also to the feeling of what is being conveyed, to the whole of it, not part of it." He understood that the most basic of all human needs is the need to understand and be understood. He didn't like talking about himself so he made it a point of getting others to talk about their interests and their concerns. This worked perfectly for Mr. Sam because human nature is such that people who are nervous have a tendency to try to hide their nervousness by talking about themselves. Sam Walton would tell you if you want to motivate others, start by developing your own listening skills; just ask an open-ended questions and let the person you're taking with do the talking. He figured out a funny thing about the motivational power of good listening skills: people like others who are willing to listen to what they have to say. It's actually counterintuitive: when you talk about yourself, you're considered a bore, but when you are a good listener, you become very popular! Mr. Sam was a great example of this in that he rarely talked about himself, but he listened to everyone around him and in the process he became an extremely popular and respected leader.
- *Using people's names* was something Mr. Sam really believed in. He even had a knack for remembering names. With so

many associates at Wal-Mart, Mr. Sam required everybody to wear a name badge with their first name proudly and prominently displayed. Sam Walton realized that a person's name is the most important sound in any language and that it is impossible to use his or her name too much. By constantly referring to people by name, you are showing you sincerely care about them as a person. The message this sends is that they are important to you. Mr. Sam realized that using an individual's name personalizes the relationship and has a tremendous motivational effect.

- *Looking people in the eye* is the sincerest way to demonstrate that they are important and that they have your full attention. The positive motivating effect is the same in all types of interactions including those in the workplace, church, school, and home. To some this communication technique may seem like a common courtesy, but we all know people who we wish would use it. It's a simple technique that involves smiling at the other person, making eye contact, and using active listening skills like nodding your head or saying "uh-huh." Mr. Sam used this technique with customers and the associates. His employees were extremely loyal to him because of his human relations skills, which motivated people to want to achieve great things.

Are you motivated to achieve at above-average performance levels? Do you want others to achieve at those levels? Are you willing to set high performance expectations for everyone? Sam Walton certainly did, and he led by example. His work ethic was legendary, and he has inspired thousands of his leadership disciples to willingly and enthusiastically work the long hours necessary to get the work done at Wal-Mart. Just as Mr. Sam thought about the business every waking hour, so do most of the company's leaders. Because it is a global business, with its stores open 24 hours a day, 7 days a week, the company's executives literally have problems to deal with around the clock and around the planet. In this fast-paced and ever-changing environment being motivated isn't optional.

It's easy for leaders in any organization to cascade down aggressive goals and objectives and to then expect their employees to deliver on them. That's the approach some leaders take, but it can have a demotivating impact on employees. The trick to getting people motivated to achieve goals is to get employees involved in helping to set the goals in the first place. Often employees aren't given the credit they deserve with regard to the intellectual horsepower they possess. Smart leaders figure out how to tap into the knowledge of their people and by doing so gain the advantage provided by team synergy. People who are involved in setting goals are more motivated to achieve them.

Sam Walton had the ability to engender fierce loyalty from his company managers and his associates. He captured their hearts and minds by never asking them to do anything he wasn't willing to do himself. He led his retailing empire the old-fashioned way, by example. Mr. Sam termed this style of leadership *servant leadership*, which simply means as a leader of people you must serve the needs of your people first. Don Soderquist, the former COO, said, "The undeniable cornerstone of Wal-Mart's success can be traced back to our strong belief in the dignity of each individual. We view our associates as much more than a pair of hands to do a job, but also as a wonderful source of new ideas."* Sam Walton

---

*From: Wal-Mart China Website
http://www.wal-martchina.com/english/walmart/culture.htm#story

realized that by showing he cared about his associate partners, they, in turn, would be motivated to do a good job.

Most of Wal-Mart's leaders are thrust into a new job at one point or another in their career in which they are clearly in over their heads. In this scenario, it's sink or swim. More often than not, individuals thrust into a job for which they weren't originally qualified accomplish the seemingly impossible. They succeed! Through personal motivation they do whatever is necessary, work whatever hours are required, seek whatever help they need from their teammates, and magically claw their way to success. Some staffing professionals would view this scenario as an impossible, one-in-a-million shot. I saw this happen over and over again. Mr. Sam's team of motivated people at Wal-Mart often made the difficult look easy and the impossible plausible every day!

When you provide average people with the chance of a lifetime, they realize how rare those chances are and they don't squander them. By believing in people more than they believed in themselves, Sam Walton facilitated miracles in people's lives. He transformed average people with what I believe is a form of self-fulfilling prophecy. He figured out that if people think they can do something, they can, and if they think they can't, they are right, they can't.

I remember a football story that illustrates this point about the importance of leaders believing in people. In a professional game with the team down by 2 points, with minutes to go, facing a fourth down and 1 yard to go on their opponents 25-yard line the coach had a decision to make. Would he kick a field goal to take the lead or go for a first down? The kick would be 42 yards and would put the team in the lead. If they were to make a 1-yard gain, they would have a first down, moving them closer to the end zone. The coach decided to go for it and the team runs the ball but gets stopped short of a first down; they are forced to turn the ball over to their opponents and lose the game. In the locker room when asked by reporters why he didn't try to kick a field goal, his response was, "I didn't believe my kicker could make it." From that point onward that kicker was no longer effective. For the rest of that season his performance deteriorated, eventually leading to his expulsion from the NFL. When he was later asked what happened to his performance, he said, "Ever since the coach had said he didn't think I could make that kick, I stopped believing in my own ability." Because his coach didn't think he could kick a field goal, this professional field goal kicker also believed he would fail. The same thing happens in the relationships between managers and employees when an employee senses a lack of faith in his or her ability from a supervisor. It's called a negative self-fulfilling prophecy.

By believing in the abilities of people more than they believe in themselves, challenging them with big-time opportunities, and stepping back and giving them the final choice to succeed or fail, Mr. Sam triggered a primal desire that was already deeply embedded in the minds of his people to compete and thrive! It's the self-fulfilling belief before you start that often determines your likelihood of success or failure.

Sam Walton, the master motivator, tapped into this reservoir of human potential and drew out human performance beyond even his own lofty expectations. By doing so, he gave his team of ordinary people the chance to achieve at extraordinary levels! By pouring themselves into their work and committing themselves day after day, month after month, those thrust into new jobs at Wal-Mart eventually solve the puzzle and never look back. Before they know it, they have not only figured out how to do the job, they master it! Just like Sam Walton, what they think about most of the time is what they become. Wal-Mart's motivated people become outstanding at what they do by hard work, a can-do attitude, and sheer determination. In the end, when someone succeeds under these difficult circumstances at Wal-Mart, no one is really surprised. Mr. Sam knew his motivated associates would succeed because he had created a positive self-fulfilling prophecy.

When I speak to audiences I often talk about the choice each individual can make to become an outstanding performer, like Sam Walton, in whatever they choose to do. All it takes is personal motivation, commitment, and hard work in order to be the best. I tell the story of the difference in baseball between having a batting average of .250 and a batting average of .333. You see a .250 hitter gets 3 hits every 12 times at bat and a .333 hitter gets 4 hits every 12 times at bat. The difference is only one hit every 12 times at bat! When you think about it, the difference isn't that much between a good hitter with a .250 average and a great hitter with a .333 average!

As in this example, the difference between good and great isn't that much in most of life's worthwhile endeavors! However, if achieving greatness were easy, everyone would do it! The key to becoming great at whatever you do is to believe in yourself and in your ability to be the best. Like Mr. Sam you have to pay the price and be willing to work harder than your competitors to reach the top of your profession. I'll end this chapter as I end many of my speeches using the following quotation which captures the spirit of the motivation required to become the best and achieve your dreams. It's called, "if you think you're beaten."

> *If you think you are beaten, you are,*
> *If you think you dare not, you don't*
> *If you'd like to win, but you think you can't,*
> *It is almost certain you won't.*

If you think you'll lose, you've lost
For out in the world we find,
Success begins with a person's will—
It's all in the state of mind.

If you think you're outclassed, you are,
You've got to think high to rise,
You've got to be sure of yourself before
You can ever win the prize.

Life's battles don't always go
To the stronger woman or man,
But sooner or later he or she who wins
Is the one who thinks they can!

—author unknown

COMMUNICATE with People and Show You Care

Mr. Sam shared as much information as he possibly could with his associates because he was convinced that once they thoroughly understood the business, they'd do whatever they could to help company leaders reach goals.

Imagine the leadership challenge faced by company leaders at Wal-Mart. Almost 7,000 stores, 120 distribution centers, operations in 15 countries, and an employee population rapidly approaching 2 million! The challenges are staggering. Retailing is a people business. Once the stores are built and the product is on the shelves, the business is transacted between customers and employees. There are somewhere in the neighborhood of 130 million customers walking into Wal-Mart's stores around the globe each and every week; a whopping 83 percent of the U.S. population shopped at a Wal-Mart or Sam's Club at least once last year! It's a 24-hour-a-day, 7-day-a-week, 365-day-a-year business. Without the willing involvement of the associates to provide solid service those customers might choose to shop elsewhere. How did Sam Walton get everyone on the team fixated on providing great service and controlling costs? He did it by being a master communicator of "one vision and one company."

Mr. Sam's fourth success secret for achieving remarkable results is *"COMMUNICATE with people and show you care."* He believed that the more the associates knew about the business and the better they understood the pressures, the more they would care. He knew they could help fix any sales, service, and cost-related problems and by doing so they could help improve those numbers. To that end, he discussed the detailed information about the key success indicators, from his confidential financial reports, with all of his people. He provided more information rather than less because he believed that information was power. As far as Sam Walton was concerned, the advantages of giving his team of business partners the confidential financial information they needed to run the business far outweighed any concerns or potential risk of leaks of that information to his competitors.

Think about how difficult it is in a company the size of Wal-Mart to just keep everyone informed of the current news in the company. A Wal-Mart store manager described the massive staff in just one Supercenter this way:

> In my store the year we opened it, we did $83 million and I had about 450 associates on the payroll and of course that number spiked during the holiday season. We had 25 hourly department managers and 11 salaried assistant managers. In addition, I had two salaried co-managers reporting to me. Including optical and pharmacy I had a total of 20 salaried people reporting to me in my store.

For Wal-Mart, having information is the difference between having the ability to adapt quickly to changes in the market and utter chaos. Without a steady stream of good information the company would be paralyzed and implode under its own weight. How does the retail giant keep all of those stores and their people up to date with the news they need? They do it by thinking small.

In other companies leaders are taught to think big, start small, and then scale up. At Wal-Mart, leaders are taught to think small, start small, and scale up. That's also how company leaders attack the communication challenge. By simplifying everything the company does and worrying about every individual store, each store has its own identity.

Let me explain. In company terms, if Wal-Mart is the universe, each store is an individual planet with its own unique problems, issues, and concerns. Its store managers are taught to think in the smallest and simplest terms possible—one store at a time, one department at a time, and one customer at a time. To accomplish this challenge home office leaders empower store managers with the responsibility and authority they need to run each store. Each store stands alone from a sales and profitability standpoint, and the management team and the associates take ownership of their own Wal-Mart store as if it were the only store in the chain. For this reason, each store manager realizes he or she owns everything that happens in and to that store. By feeding information to the store managers and training them to disseminate that information every day, the company's field managers and associates at locations around the world are kept informed of the news they need.

Communicate, communicate, communicate is the standard to which Wal-Mart's leaders are held. As the largest company in the world with a new store opening every day of the year somewhere in the world, Wal-Mart's leaders are saddled with a huge communication challenge. Company leaders attack this challenge via a variety of methods, including live satellite broadcasts, Wal-Mart TV and radio, a company newsletter called *Wal-Mart World*, the company Web site, e-mail, company training programs, an open door policy, employee opinion surveys, an employee handbook, and daily "stand-up" communication meetings in every Wal-Mart store.

They use their own satellite broadcasting studio to send out live and prerecorded news to the stores. They also have a radio station. The company has the ability to broadcast live radio or TV simultaneously to the entire chain of stores, or if there is a need, they can send a broadcast to an individual store. This technique was used at sites experiencing union organizing when Sam Walton was alive. Mr. Sam would sit in the Wal-Mart broadcast studio in Bentonville and talk to the associates on live TV or radio. When Mr. Sam was done presenting his message to the associates, the union's organizing drive always failed. This same approach to communication is used by merchandise buyers to communicate seasonal product strategies to department heads across all of the stores. Human resources, what Wal-Mart terms the *people division*, used live and prerecorded TV to get messages out to the associates about compensation and benefit issues important to them.

Wal-Mart also uses its intranet and the Internet to communicate with the stores, distribution centers, home office, and other outlying locations. Store managers participate in a telephone conference call every Saturday conducted by their district manager who shares the latest company news from across the world.

At the daily stand-up meetings, which are sort of like a huddle used in a football game, manager/associate two-way communication is encouraged. Associates are invited to ask questions about issues concerning their jobs or the operation. Updates are given to everyone about the latest news impacting the company or the local store. Stand-up meetings are just that and typically last only 5 to 10 minutes based on whether it is a busy or slow news day and the number of questions asked by associates. In many cases the meetings are held out in the open in the front of the store near the cash registers in plain view of customers. Discussion topics include "opening the books" and sharing what other companies might consider proprietary information, including letting the associates know where their store stands on sales and profitability. These meetings are held daily, and in a 24-hour store, are held with each shift. Typically, the discussion focuses around sales from the previous day and specifically how each department is performing against sales forecasts. The manager leading the meeting talks about various areas of the business and even openly discusses associate concerns. This is just one example of the extraordinary lengths to which Wal-Mart will go to make certain its associates are kept informed about important issues and news impacting their work lives.

Top managers of the company, who work at the headquarters, are required to attend an important information and communication meeting every Saturday morning starting at 7:00 A.M. Originated by Mr. Sam, Wal-Mart's Saturday morning meeting has become famous throughout the world of business. Held at the company's home office in Bentonville, Arkansas, this executive lead meeting, attended by 500 of Wal-Mart's top leaders, provides real–time two-way communication of Wal-Mart's competitive strategies and tactics. Held in the company's corporate auditorium, the meeting is one part pep rally, including a company cheer, one part fun with a dash of humor, and one part business. The information discussed is lively and unscripted with everyone encouraged to provide input to the debate. Executives, managers, and supervisors from every headquarters functional area participate in the adjustment of corporate strategies and tactics using current fresh market intelligence gathered by executives who have been out traveling in the stores earlier in the week.

This forum provides Wal-Mart's leaders with the flexibility to reevaluate and adjust company strategies and tactics each and every Saturday as conditions change in the marketplace. On Saturday afternoon new directives go out to stores around the world and may already be implemented on Monday morning when the executives of Wal-Mart's competitors return to their offices. For this reason, Wal-Mart's Saturday morning meetings have become a formidable competitive advantage for the company in the marketplace. This level of communication and flexibility is unusual for a company the size of Wal-Mart, giving them the ability to turn their aircraft carrier of a company nimbly like a PT boat.

One of the merchandise buyers explained the typical workweek for a buyer and how they communicated with one another when they weren't traveling to the stores:

My work schedule at Wal-Mart's headquarters is a five-and-a-half day workweek. I go in early every day at about 6:00 A.M. in the morning and about 10 to 15 percent of the buyers also go in about that time. We get together first thing and discuss our numbers for that particular week. Throughout the day we spend time on the telephone, do planning, and have meetings with the vendors. You finish up your day 12 hours later around 6:00 P.M. and you'd work that schedule Monday through Friday. Then, on Saturday we come in at around 7:00 A.M., get our sales figures, and head for the auditorium for the Saturday morning meeting. All of the executives of the company, regional staffs, and buyers discuss how that particular week had finished as of Friday. We discuss what areas are doing well, which areas aren't, and why. We talk about particular merchandising issues that have come up and try to develop solutions or ideas to solve them on the spot. If we don't have an answer, we find it and get back to people.

Mr. Sam's Saturday morning meetings emphasized communication and problem solving, and it is this forum that really pulls all of the departments together into one cohesive organization. Fluid communication between departments is one of the more important secrets to the success of Wal-Mart.

To understand Mr. Sam's communication style, you have to understand the personality of Sam Walton. He was always tinkering with things, changing things, and improving things. He was a lifelong learner who was fixated on improving everything around him. His passion for his business and his compassion for people are the two attributes that really set him apart from most leaders. Mr. Sam never lost the common touch, and he ran his business using good old-fashioned common sense.

He had a disarming personality. People felt comfortable walking right up and talking to him as if he were an old friend. He was one of those rare people who had the ability to immediately establish rapport with everyone he met. Customers or employees, Mr. Sam was interested in knowing what was on their mind, especially their opinions of his stores. He gave you the feeling when he talked with you that you were the most important person in the world to him at that moment. Once you had met him, you knew you had met someone who was really special.

A former store manager shared this insight with me about his first meeting with Sam Walton:

> I remember the first time I met Sam Walton; I was an assistant manager in a store in Georgia at the time. Mr. Sam arrived at the store unannounced; he had flown his plane there that morning from who knows where. He walked in the door when we opened up for associates at 7:00 A.M., and that was back in the days when we opened to the public at 9:00 A.M. He spent some time walking the floor and visiting with all of the associates. He decided to have a store meeting with all of the associates, so he called everybody up front. He had everybody sit on the floor in the front of the store by the registers. He got down on his knees and talked to us about how important customer service was and how we had to take care of the customers. He made people feel good about themselves. He was down to earth, a real good ole boy who gave you the feeling that he didn't have any more than anybody else in the world had. He brought himself down to the people's level by dealing with them, and talking with them, which made everyone feel comfortable and at ease talking with him. You felt like you could ask him anything in the world and not be ridiculed or criticized for asking him. We got through with the meeting and of course we did the Wal-Mart cheer and then he went back to walking the floor.

Clearly, when you met Sam Walton, you knew you had met someone who was truly unique. So what are the personality traits that made him so unique and so successful? Here are some adjectives that come to mind that best describe him: honest, competitive, courageous, caring, hard working, cheap, driven, disciplined, curious, humble, stubborn, decisive, and ambitious. He could also be described as: street smart, team oriented, a developer of people, tight fisted with a buck, a tough negotiator, a great communicator, and an aggressive competitor. He was a fact finder, not a fault finder. In his role as a leader, his approach would change to suit the current set of circumstances including: servant leader, trailblazer, risk taker, change agent, chief merchant, storytelling pontificator, teacher, team builder, entrepreneur, visionary leader, theatrical performer, motivational expert, comedian, psychologist, and preacher. He was a master of the art of communication.

Once Wal-Mart stock was issued and it became a publicly traded company, reporters made their way to Bentonville in droves to do stories on Sam Walton's success. He'd have nothing to do with those reporters, but he was hounded everywhere he went. They'd follow him around town to see where he went and to see what he did. They'd find him eating at a Shoney's Restaurant or getting his hair cut at the barbershop on the square in Bentonville. He was confounded by the question from a reporter who quizzically asked him, "Why do you get your haircut at a barbershop?" In frustration Mr. Sam responded, "Where else would I get a haircut?"

Imagine a billionaire who drives a pickup truck, wears a baseball cap, eats at Shoney's, gets his haircut at the local barbershop, and lives in a modest house, that's Sam Walton. He was a good old country boy who loved to go hunting with his dogs, but at the same time he was a business genius. Sam Walton was to retailing what Michael Jordan was to basketball, an absolute master of his art. If Jordan was the "king of the court," Walton was the "merchant prince of the retailing world."

One of Sam Walton's great passions was getting out to the stores to speak with his customers and to communicate his cultural message directly to his associates. Because he was a pilot, he was known for flying his own plane out to stores to drop in without prior notice. One of Wal-Mart's store managers related a memorable story about a time when Mr. Sam did just that by visiting his store in Alabama:

> I got a page to come up to the customer service desk and when I arrived there was Sam Walton. I'd met him several times and knew who he was as soon as I saw him. I had heard from my district manager that he might be in the area, but you never knew if he'd actually come to your store as he had so many stores to choose from. Mr. Sam remembered me immediately and after shaking my hand he asked why I hadn't arranged for someone to pick him up at the airport. I told him I was unaware of his intended visit and that I surely would have picked him up had I known he was coming. With him that day was an old man and Mr. Sam directed me to pay him for giving him a ride to the store from the local airport. As it turned out Sam Walton didn't have his wallet, credit cards, or any cash with him so I paid the man out of our petty cash account. The old man said he was driving past the airport and found Mr. Sam hitchhiking on the road in front of the airport, so he had stopped to pick him up. He had no idea that the Sam he had picked up was THE Sam Walton who was the founder of Wal-Mart!

His forays out into the stores are legendary. Each and every week of the year Mr. Sam would venture out into the stores without a strict itinerary and visit stores with little fanfare or planning. His goal was to come back at the end of the week to Bentonville with fresh market intelligence to share with the company's leadership team so they could plan their competitive strategies. All

Wal-Mart executives, as well as the company's buying staff, also visited the stores. Each week they would fly, in one of Wal-Mart's propeller-driven airplanes, with a professional pilot at the helm, to markets across the country to visit competitor's stores, meet with Wal-Mart's associates and talk with customers. Mr. Sam believed that information is power and that current and actionable information is real power. Wal-Mart's market intelligence remains one of the company's strategic and tactical competitive advantages.

Mr. Sam used to say, "You can't 'merchandise the world' by sitting in your office." One of the merchandise buyers from the home office in Bentonville reflected on the importance of traveling to the stores:

> I traveled to stores 25 to 30 percent of the time. Once a year all of the buyers would go out and work in the stores for 5 days between Thanksgiving and Christmas. You could pick any store in the country and you'd work the entire store, helping put up stock, clean up, and help customers. At that time of the year the stores were particularly busy so any help they could get was appreciated. I visited a store in a small town in Oklahoma that I had never been to before and to get there I drove 4 or 5 hours. They were all excited to have someone from the corporate office and by physically helping the people at the stores, that inspired people and created camaraderie with the home office, sort of a "one big team" philosophy.
>
> Throughout the year, the buyers would travel with the regional operations staff to the stores. Because they were located at the home office, every week they would go out and travel and they'd take two, three, or four buyers with them. Every buyer had their own category so they'd check out their own category in the store and see if there were any problems we could help the stores with and it would help us to get to know the other side. You couldn't do your job well as a buyer if you didn't know the circumstances in the stores. Traveling to the stores improved overall communications.

Mr. Sam taught company leaders that when you are fired up about your business, your people will follow suit and they too will get fired up! He worked tirelessly to communicate his standards and values to everyone in the organization and by doing so he transferred his enthusiasm to others. Mr. Sam came up with a unique strategy for communicating his standards and values through storytelling.

One of Sam Walton's more interesting strategies was his use of folklore to proliferate his company's culture. Mr. Sam was a master storyteller, and he used rich cultural stories to drive home key points about his sales, service, and expense control philosophies and to reinforce his business standards. Many of the stories he liked the best were told and retold to reinforce important cultural messages. By telling simple and easy-to-remember stories over and over again, he avoided the potential for communication overload. The belief was that people will forget the details of what you tell them, but they'll always remember the great stories. The history of the culture of the company is anchored forever in those stories. His stories were usually fun, always memorable, and typically were about a significant contribution of one of the associates. His use of storytelling was a primary method of communicating standards to both managers and associates at the company.

Wal-Mart and Sam's Club also use rituals to communicate their cultural beliefs. One of those rituals is the Wal-Mart cheer. The cheer is used during group meetings of associates as a way to show team spirit and loyalty. It's also a way to focus everyone on the importance of customer service. The use of folklore, storytelling, and rituals is one of the most interesting tactics of Mr. Sam's grand plan for communication.

How did he get his company leaders and managers to embrace his standards for communication? Mr. Sam did it by developing a set of 11 key leadership competencies and then communicating his standards. These key leadership competencies were selected from a list of about 100. This meant Sam Walton and his executive team selected only 11 competencies upon which to focus to the exclusion of all the rest on that list. Mr. Sam was directly involved in the final selection of Wal-Mart's key leadership competencies, which he divided into two areas—one he called *people skills* and the other he called *work processes:*

People Skills	Work Processes
Communication	Continuous improvement
Developing others	Sense of urgency
Motivating others	Team development
Customer focus	Organization/planning
Listening	Expectations/accountability
	Resolving problems

Identifying these 11 key leadership competencies allowed Wal-Mart's executives to uniformly communicate both standards and expectations to all of the company's managers and supervisors. The following provides a description of each of Mr. Sam's key leadership people skills and work processes.

PEOPLE SKILLS

Communication

With hundreds of associates in every store, company managers have a major role in uniformly communicating company performance and cultural standards to Wal-Mart's associates. Imagine the challenge of implementing even the simplest directives in an organization with so many people and locations geographically spread out across the globe. Mr. Sam wanted customers to walk into each and every one of his stores and have the same positive experience at each. This meant his cultural standards had to be consistent around the world. The only way to accomplish such a daunting task is by aggressively communicating with everyone on the team. His managers were responsible for providing the associates with the help, information, and motivation they needed to run the day-to-day operation of the business.

He felt it was important for everyone to understand what was going on around them so that they could help solve problems. For Mr. Sam's team truly to be successful, he knew that every member had to be engaged, participate, and understand the game plan. He viewed communication as a two-way street and placed great importance on the input of his associates. For this reason, it was important for his associates to know what was going on in the company, and it was important for them to have a voice. Mr. Sam devised a strategy requiring daily stand-up meetings in every store and distribution center every day. In the 24-hour locations that could mean as many as three meetings a day to cover all three shifts. By requiring daily meetings, Mr. Sam was able to ensure that his team of associates was constantly updated on what was going on around them and given the confidence to do their jobs.

Developing Others

The ability to staff the growth of Wal-Mart has always been a concern to Sam Walton. With new stores opening almost every day, the need for qualified people is virtually insatiable. In order to avoid diluting his company culture with new people from other companies, he had to find a way to replicate his own company's culture. His solution was to train his own people to assume promotional opportunities. Developing the talents and potential of his own associates and then promoting them from within has proven to be a critical component in the achievement of Wal-Mart's growth strategies. In some ways Mr. Sam viewed hiring and developing talent as *the* primary job responsibility of every leader in his company. For this reason, Wal-Mart managers have a dual role in developing people. First, they are expected to teach and train associates for their current jobs. Even more importantly, their second role is to prepare associates to take on more responsibility and become the company's future leaders. It was quite common for Sam Walton to move associates successfully between functions in the home office into jobs for which the associates involved had little or no prerequisite experience. He believed and proved that by cross-training of associates throughout the organization, he ensured the availability of a pool of internally promotable candidates as promotional opportunities became available.

Motivating Others

One of the most difficult jobs of a Wal-Mart store manager or distribution center manager is balancing the needs of the business against the needs of the associates. Mr. Sam expected his leaders to figure out how to achieve this precarious balance. He believed a manager's true success is measured by his or her ability and desire to help all of the other associates on the team to be as successful as they can be. When the associates sensed or felt their manager was looking out for their interests the associates would in turn look out for the interests of the company. Mr. Sam preached, emphasized, and taught the importance of having strong people skills. For the most part, the individuals Mr. Sam promoted into higher levels of responsibility were the leaders who had the proven ability to work with and motivate a large team of people.

Customer Focus

The belief in using an outside-in approach to the selection of products offered to customers is part of the original strategy Mr. Sam used at the beginning of his career. As he visited his own stores, he would talk to his own customers and ask them for ideas about the kinds of products he should carry. He also visited the stores of his competitors in search of new product ideas he could take back to Wal-Mart. Greeting customers, approaching them in the store, and helping them find what they are looking for are all elements of the superior customer service that is the cornerstone of Mr. Sam's service philosophy. He learned some of his lessons about customer standards from Stew Leonard, a grocery store owner, operator, and founder in New England. Leonard was a pioneer in the use of customer focus groups and his store, Stew Leonard's, exceeded industry standards in sales and service. His service mantra is "Our mission is to create happy customers...by selling the freshest products at the best prices in a friendly, fun atmosphere!" Mr. Sam liked the way Stew Leonard communicated his standards for "no questions asked" product guarantees so much that he added one of Leonard's service sayings to Wal-Mart's customer service training programs. Leonard's two rules of customer service are

Rule 1: The customer is always right.
Rule 2: If the customer is wrong...refer to rule 1.

Mr. Sam communicated this saying as a standard for service to his management team and all associates. This customer service standard remains in place to this day.

Listening

Mr. Sam believed the relationship with his associates needed to be a partnership. To accomplish that goal required good communication and a continuous exchange of ideas. It also meant listening to the ideas, constructive criticism, and feedback from the associates. He felt it was very important to listen to the associates and he insisted upon open, free, and honest communication up and down the organization. He felt it was important to visit people where they worked and to talk to them where they were most comfortable. When disputes or problems did arise, Mr. Sam was always a fact finder, not a fault finder, and he encouraged associates to use the company's open door policy to get their issues addressed and resolved. Mr. Sam encouraged associates to come up with new ideas and new ways of doing things. He was the first to admit that many of the best ideas currently in use around his company had come from the associates themselves.

WORK PROCESSES

Continuous Improvement

One of the pillars of total quality established by Sam Walton at Wal-Mart was the concept of continuous improvement. Good was never good enough to Mr. Sam and he encouraged everyone to improve all of Wal-Mart's many work processes. Sam Walton had no sacred cows. Every process, procedure, and policy was subject to scrutiny and potential recommendations for improvement. The goal was always to reduce the amount of time necessary to complete tasks and reduce the amount of effort required. Small improvements in one location could easily be replicated in locations around the world. A small local improvement had the potential for a big impact worldwide.

Sense of Urgency

In my office at the Wal-Mart headquarters, I had a poster on the wall called the "Sundown Rule," which addressed the company standard for getting things done. It is like having an antiprocrastination policy. The Sundown Rule requires everyone in the company to follow up on any and all requests they've received from the stores or fellow associates before going home each day. With the size of the company and the number of stores, distribution centers, and associates, achieving the lofty standards of the Sundown Rule was easier said then done. The pace created as a result of this standard was nothing short of frenetic, with everyone focused on getting things done now. Often, the level of communication between people and departments would actually increase as the day went on! The Sundown Rule was an important component of Mr. Sam's internal customer service standard.

Team Development

Teamwork is a way of life at Wal-Mart. Company managers spend a great deal of time facilitating cooperation between people and departments. Sort of like a basketball team each individual is expected to play his or her position while working together and to back up their teammates as opportunities arise. Mr. Sam understood the power of synergistic teamwork, and his goal was to achieve synergy. The basic premise behind synergistic teams at Wal-Mart is this: A group of 10 individuals working separately without communicating will perform at a lower level than a similar group of 10 who communicate with one another and work together. Wal-Mart's associates are generalists not specialists, and you won't hear its associates say, "That's not my job!" Many organizations are missing the opportunity to achieve team synergy by failing to get their employees to work together and communicate with one another in a spirit of true cooperation.

Organization/Planning

Everything at Wal-Mart is big. The stores can be over 200,000 square feet and the distribution centers over a million square feet with tens of thousands of products and tractor trailer loads of new product arriving daily. Add to the mix the challenge of coordinating thousands of suppliers and almost 2 million of its own associates and you can see the importance of organization and planning. Coupled with the stores being open 24 hours a day, with three shifts of associates, company managers are dealing with a whole lot of moving parts. In this hectic environment the ability to organize and plan so many activities can be the difference between a well-run business and total chaos. Running a massive Supercenter or Distribution Center truly is a team effort and can only be accomplished with the cooperation and involvement of everyone working together. To that end, it is vitally important for company managers to stay organized by developing daily and weekly business plans and to communicate those plans to everyone involved.

Expectations/Accountability

As the title of the introduction to this book proclaims, high expectations are the key to everything at Wal-Mart. Mr. Sam always believed in setting goals out of easy reach but never out of sight. He often admitted that the success he was able to achieve as a result of the efforts of his associates had exceeded his expectations. A master of creating a self-fulfilling prophecy, Mr. Sam challenged teams of people to achieve at levels they didn't believe possible and more often than not they'd meet or exceed his optimistic expectations. If you hold people accountable for achieving average goals, they'll achieve at average levels; however, what Mr. Sam found is if you hold them accountable to above-average goals, a group of ordinary people, working together, can achieve at the highest levels. They'll often surprise their own leaders with their ability to perform. That's the power of high expectations, accountability, and team synergy at Wal-Mart.

Resolving Problems

Mr. Sam believed in spending his time solving problems, not in wasting his time trying to fix blame. With the volume of issues cropping up constantly he didn't have time to think any other way. When problems did occur, he expected everyone to jump in to help. Managers often pull together groups of associates to discuss their ideas of how to handle a given situation to get their opinions and to implement a strategy for resolution. Mr. Sam often said it's the associates closest to the work who always have the best solutions to problems. The associates at Wal-Mart are empowered to resolve all kinds of problems, including merchandise returns for cash and product exchanges, without getting managers involved. The speed with which they are able to resolve issues is a testament to their teamwork, can-do attitude, work ethic, and sense of urgency. By the way, Mr. Sam viewed problems as opportunities.

One of the more interesting communication standards Mr. Sam used was called *telling the truth*. Because his goal wasn't to find and punish the guilty, Wal-Mart's managers and associates were expected to openly discuss problems with a focus on solving them. Posturing, positioning, or spinning answers was perceived as a waste of time. The Wal-Mart way has always been to just answer questions truthfully. I always found this approach refreshing. Interestingly enough, for Sam Walton, who had nothing to hide, telling the truth actually worked. His company culture was based on integrity, making solving company problems much easier.

To the outside observer, Wal-Mart's high-performing culture is one of the great mysteries of the company. Many ask why someone getting paid retail wages would care so much about their job and their company. The fact is most of the associates at Wal-Mart really do care about the company and their jobs. They take tremendous ownership and pride in their Wal-Mart Store, Sam's Club, or Distribution Center. But why? It's not any one thing Mr. Sam put in place; it's many things. It's promotional opportunities and emphasis on teams. It's having managers who care about their fellow associates like a Wal-Mart family. It's average people being given the opportunity few companies in America would offer to them. All of this coupled with company profit sharing drives Wal-Mart's average people to become fanatical about the success of their company. In the process, the associates who are hired with average skills are motivated to achieve at above-average levels of performance. Wal-Mart quite literally gets *more from less* by drawing out the full potential of individuals and teams. With respect to achieving high performance from ordinary people, Mr. Sam figured out the greatest success secret of all by communicating with his associates like they were his business partners!

APPRECIATE and Recognize People for Their Efforts and Results

Sam Walton liked to showcase examples
of associates who had accomplished
something terrific, which he would then
communicate to everyone else in
the company as a benchmark
or standard. He knew that if one
associate could do it, then
all could do it!

I can remember attending the Saturday morning meetings when Sam Walton was still personally running the meetings. On one particular Saturday I knew when I arrived that Mr. Sam intended to go hunting later that day because his hunting dog cages were in the back of his old pickup truck. As it turned out, he had taken his bird dogs inside the building that morning and had released them to run in the halls of the headquarters. When he walked out onto the stage, he was already dressed head to toe in camouflaged hunting gear, with a matching camouflaged Wal-Mart baseball cap on his head and his clipboard in hand. He obviously didn't want to waste a minute getting ready to go out bird hunting as soon as the meeting ended.

This particular morning he talked about a topic he often focused on, which was the associates in the stores. What he said that morning stuck with me for all these years: "The folks on the front line— the ones who actually talk to the customers—are the only ones who really know what's going on out there. You'd better find out what they know." Every week Mr. Sam stood at that Saturday morning meeting and virtually every week he'd discuss a similar belief about the importance of the associates in the stores and distribution centers, and also the truck drivers, to the success of the company.

Sam Walton's fifth success secret for achieving remarkable results is *"APPRECIATE and recognize people for their efforts and results."* To do that, he believed in often praising the accomplishments of his associates publicly. He repeated the same message to his company leaders and to the associates themselves about the importance of people to the company's success, every week of the year. He truly did appreciate everything his associates did for the business, and they knew it! Mr. Sam realized paychecks, merit increases, and profit sharing alone aren't enough to build the kind of loyalty from the associates he wanted; people have to know you appreciate them as individuals. All of us, whether we are paid a salary or an hourly wage, like to hear that someone at a higher level in the organization appreciates our efforts and our results. Mr. Sam openly praised those who deserved it, and by doing so he created sales, service, and expense control heroes as positive examples or role models for others.

As a keynote speaker, I often speak at conferences where I present a program called "What I Learned from Sam Walton: How to Compete, Survive and Thrive in a Wal-Mart World." Usually, there is a question-and-answer session immediately following my presentation. One of the most common questions I get has to do with Wal-Mart's treatment of its own people based on news accounts audience members have seen or read. I answer these questions in the context of what I know about Sam Walton's beliefs and what I heard him teach the leadership team. Mr. Sam had Golden Rule values, which meant that he treated people the way he himself would want to be treated. He taught the company's executives, managers, and associates to do the same in their dealings with one another, with suppliers, and with the customers. Here are the thoughts shared with me by a former Wal-Mart store manager who was extremely interested in coming to the defense of Sam Walton and Wal-Mart on this issue. In telling me, he stated he was interested, as he put it, "in setting the record straight":

> It's frustrating for me to see the kinds of negative things reported about Wal-Mart in the media. A lot of it is inaccurate; don't get me wrong, Wal-Mart has its share of problems, but I think the kinds of things you are reading out in the news media today aren't the real problems at Wal-Mart. Inaccurate portrayals include: discrimination in its hiring practices, not fairly promoting from within, taking advantage of its associates by expecting them to work in unfair conditions, and requiring them to work off the clock.

What frustrates me is that the media portray that these kinds of things are commonly practiced out there and that Wal-Mart's managers regularly do those kinds of things. I know for a fact that those things are not true. Anybody who was willing to take on responsibility and accept responsibility, it was there for you to take. It wasn't spoon-fed to you; the company didn't run around looking for people and asking them to take on responsibility. But responsibility was there for anybody from a cart pusher to a department manager to take on and if they wanted to take it on and grow, the future was limitless.

The fact is that when a company becomes the largest in the world, as Wal-Mart has become, media coverage, lawsuits, and scrutiny by outsiders become a daily event. I believe the vast majority of Wal-Mart's current leaders embrace the philosophies of Sam Walton. If you look closely, often the negative coverage of Wal-Mart and its leaders is driven by special-interest groups with an axe to grind and typically highlights a local example of an individual manager or associate who has "strayed off the reservation" or committed an illegal act that is clearly contrary to Wal-Mart's published corporate policies and directives, as taught by Mr. Sam himself. The scrutiny of the company will obviously continue and the debate will go on, but I can tell you that what I learned from Sam Walton about the treatment of people and what I see in the news media are often on opposite ends of the spectrum. As I tell the audiences when I speak at conferences, Mr. Sam appreciated and valued people and believed that his associates were the key to the success of Wal-Mart.

Sam Walton was a big believer in getting out of his office and out with the troops. He practiced MBWA, which is commonly referred to as *Management By Walking Around*" or what Mr. Sam was accused of, which was *Management By Wandering Around*. If you recall, MBWA was one of those "program de jour" hot and trendy management ideas not that long ago. Most companies and leaders tried it for a while and then moved on to the next best management trend coming down the line. Wal-Mart's leaders stuck with it and they continue to practice MBWA to this day. Like this simple idea, sometimes the best ideas leaders are already aware of and they may even have used in the past and forgotten. You may want to revisit MBWA as an employee relations strategy yourself!

Mr. Sam believed in going out to his stores and distribution centers and separating himself from the site managers so he could wander around to spend private one-on-one time with the associates. He told company managers that when you're doing MBWA, don't go up to associates to discuss business, go up and ask the associates about their family, their husband, or their wife or kids. MBWA provides an opportunity to let people know how much you appreciate them. Mr. Sam believed in getting to know people one-on-one. He felt that unless people believed that you really cared about them as individuals, you only capture their "hands, not their hearts and their minds." This is one of the secrets to Mr. Sam's own success in dealing with people. When people sense how much you care about them as individuals, they'll reciprocate by showing how much they care about their jobs and their customers. Once leaders are able to capture the hearts and the minds of their employees, great things have a chance to happen.

Mr. Sam believed in recognizing the accomplishments of people, and he did it often. I think the thing he liked best about the use of recognition as a tool is the fact that it is free. He taught everyone around him by his own example. Almost every week of the year he'd talk with company leaders about someone who had gone the extra yard for the customers or achieved a safety goal or some similar accomplishment. He took it upon himself as a personal mission to create a recognition culture at Wal-Mart in which company leaders clearly proved they value the contributions of people. He didn't like to receive recognition personally, but he loved to give it to everyone else.

He believed in accentuating the positive behaviors of associates publicly and eliminating their negative behaviors in one-on-one discussions behind closed doors. He expected managers to wander around looking for noteworthy accomplishments to highlight in their daily meetings held with associates. So many organizations are good at *catching people doing things wrong.* Many even have excellent training in how to deal with those who aren't performing properly. Sam Walton believed in *catching people doing things right!* He'd school his top 500 managers at the Saturday morning meetings by teaching his own version of a One-Minute-Manager seminar on how to properly publicly reinforce the positive or the correct behaviors of associates. He'd also talk about the importance of simultaneously coaching those associates who weren't performing.

By identifying the associates who were demonstrating the correct behaviors and showcasing those accomplishments for all to see, he believed in creating local heroes in the stores, distribution centers, and fleet. These walking and talking examples of great sales, service, or expense control success stories were publicly recognized to reinforce the desired behavior. By talking about great performers in a team setting, Wal-Mart gets out the same message about what it takes to be successful at the company. Here's a story of recognition I received from a former Wal-Mart store manager:

> You can take on as much ownership and responsibility at Wal-Mart as you want to; there is nothing holding you back. As an example, one of the college students who worked part time was in charge of assembling bicycles. I decided to put him in charge of managing the entire bicycle department; he was responsible for the sales and merchandising of bicycles. One day he came

to me with a catalog featuring $200 mountain bikes, which price-wise, back then, was outrageous! He said, 'I think these will sell and I'd like to order some for our store. I've talked to a lot of people at the university who said they would buy these expensive bikes.' As the store manager, I said to him, 'I've given you ownership, now I have to trust you with it. Go ahead and order what you want to order and let's see how they sell.' Wal-Mart now sells all kinds of high-end bicycles, but it was that store and that bicycle department that was the first to do it. This young man was the first one in the entire company to push the envelope with those high-end bicycles. He did it by taking ownership of it. Every month he would remerchandise the bicycle department in order to feature a new bicycle. All of this happened as a result of his ownership of the bicycle department. This is an example of someone who took an interest in merchandising and took ownership of it. Very few companies will give a part-timer that kind of ownership in their business, but Wal-Mart does it every day. I shared this ownership success story with everyone in the store, and it served as a great way to highlight the important role every associate can play in building the business. In this particular example the associate received a monetary award in addition to recognition. Imagine the impact this one idea from a part-time associate had on company sales across the entire chain of stores once this idea was implemented everywhere else. This is a terrific example of the power of taking ownership and publicly recognizing the accomplishments of people.

Some have accused Sam Walton of having a degree in psychology in addition to his degree in economics because of his uncanny ability to understand how to motivate people. He intuitively understood that people crave recognition and that ordinary people need to feel a sense of achievement. He took the position that almost everyone wants to do a good job, regardless of the type of work they do. His managers played a pivotal role in reinforcing the feeling in associates that it does matter whether they do a good job today and that the company was counting on them to do their job to the best of their ability. Mr. Sam taught everyone that the associates who make a difference need to be recognized for their efforts and results. By understanding that people want to experience the feelings associated with the successful completion of a job, that they truly desire the feelings of ownership for their work, and that they take pride in their work area, he was able to challenge his associates to find solutions to business-related problems. Even more importantly, he empowered the associates who originally came up with an idea to champion their own idea, as only a business owner would, and implement it. He realized that ideas are the easy part of any strategy; it's the implementation of those ideas that often proves difficult or even impossible. Mr. Sam knew that associates who feel ownership and empowerment have the drive to prove to the company and to themselves that as leaders they can find and implement solutions to problems without the necessity for management intervention.

A smart manager will give employees who feel strongly about a solution to a problem, a new idea, or a product or service recommendation the opportunity to show what they can do. More often than not, where there is a will or a passion to get something done, there is often a way to get it done. Once the hard work is done and the goal has been accomplished, now all the manager needs to do is hold that accomplishment up as an example for all to see! Sincere appreciation for a job well done can go a long, long way toward building the confidence and self-esteem of the entire workforce.

Those associates who were willing to take on more responsibility were often rewarded and recognized with promotions to department manager, assistant manager, or even store manager positions.

Everyone at Wal-Mart has an equal opportunity to take on more responsibility. There is an unlimited supply of unsolved problems and untapped resources waiting for an associate who is willing to take the initiative to tackle them. For individuals who are willing to go above and beyond their day-to-day responsibilities to improve some aspect of the operation, the sky's the limit from a career standpoint. The vast majority of those in leadership positions at Wal-Mart were promoted from within. Mr. Sam valued experience at Wal-Mart much more than he valued experience from other companies. He liked people who knew and understood the Wal-Mart way of doing things. He wanted to reward people who were dedicated and loyal to the company. For this reason, if an average associate exhibited leadership traits and enjoyed taking on responsibility, he or she often got promoted. There were and still are plenty of great promotional opportunities available for associates who prove through their efforts and results that they've got the right stuff.

It has been said, "Be careful what you wish for because you might get it!" That's what I thought of when someone talked about getting promoted at Wal-Mart. You see, promotional opportunities are readily available to those willing to take the initiative; the struggle for those newly promoted into positions of more responsibility is in proving they are equal to the challenge. The standard Mr. Sam set for everything was daunting. The learning curve for leaders, just to get up to speed, is very steep, but unfortunately the time available to do so is limited. The Wal-Mart way of doing things demands extraordinary commitment, hard work, long hours, and attention to detail that some people simply are unwilling or unable to give. With high expectations being the key to everything, it seems like everything is a priority. Managers have to exceed customers' expectations, keep the shelves stocked, get customers through the checkouts quickly, and do it all with the lowest possible budget. Often this means lean staffing and not enough hands to get the work done. Extra work, which in many companies would get done by bringing in temps or having employees work overtime, gets done by salaried managers who need to do whatever it takes to get the job done. Payroll budgets are strictly monitored and the standard for paying overtime rates is zero! The pace is always frenetic. For obvious reasons, those who are promoted have to have an extraordinary level of commitment and a high sense of urgency in order to succeed.

Sam Walton's top leadership team didn't receive perks like the executives of many organizations. Nobody had a lavishly appointed office, designated parking space, country club membership, or company car. There was no executive dining room or private bathrooms. Even coffee and donuts had to be purchased! As far as Mr. Sam was concerned, every associate was equally important to the success of the company and deserved to be treated in the same manner. He believed you can't say one thing as a leader while doing another, so if he wanted to place expense control demands on everyone else, he and the other executives had to set the example. If the company required those who traveled to stay two to a room in budget hotels when they traveled, so would the executives; what was fair for one was fair for all. Everyone else had to fly coach class and so did Sam Walton. Imagine a billionaire flying on a commercial airline and sitting in a coach class seat! That was Mr. Sam leading by example. Treating everyone the same in this regard was Mr. Sam's sincere way of proving to everyone that all associates were equally important to the company.

One of the great cultural secrets of dealing with employees that I learned from Mr. Sam is really no big secret at all: Employees share many of the exact same goals and aspirations that their supervisors and managers do in life. Wal-Mart's employees and your employees want to:

- Have their opinions taken seriously
- Be treated with respect by their supervisors
- Be recognized when they do a good job
- Be a member of a winning team
- Have the responsibility and authority to get a job done
- Be given positive and not-so-positive performance feedback
- Have a supervisor who listens and uses their ideas
- "Feel in on things" going on around them in the organization
- Provide for their families, pay the rent, and send their kids to college
- Receive training and development so they can do their current job well
- Receive preparation for potential promotional opportunities
- Know their efforts are appreciated and rewarded

The realization that everyone is motivated by the similar goals in life fit right into Mr. Sam's strategy for building his business. By focusing on helping others achieve their goals, he was able to focus them on helping him build his company. In many cases all Mr. Sam did was provide an opportunity for people to succeed, and that's precisely what they did. Mr. Sam was always quick to recognize his associates as the single most important and defining reason for Wal-Mart's overwhelming success around the world.

Sam Walton figured out long ago that employee behavior, which is reinforced, has a tendency to be repeated. Wal-Mart's employees are no different than those in other organizations; all employees need to receive feedback and encouragement in order to continue doing a good job. Mr. Sam proved over and over again that by using feedback and praise his associates could be molded into high-performing team members.

Some companies treat their employees like mushrooms; they keep them in the dark and they feed them . . . fertilizer! Often, after a brief orientation period, employees are left on their own, with little feedback from their supervisor. Not at Wal-Mart, where its associates continue to receive feedback throughout their career. Following this logic, all of your employees who are poor, good, very good, and excellent performers need to receive feedback to ensure more positive performance in the future. In other words, like Sam Walton, accentuate and recognize positive effort and results and eliminate negative performance and behaviors.

Treating employees with dignity and respect is the Sam Walton way. That's not to say that nonperformers are allowed to run amok. The company has aggressive expectations for dealing with nonperforming employees. In some companies, supervisors are hesitant to deal with those employees with job performance- or attendance-related problems. Why is this? I think it is human nature. Nobody likes to have to tell somebody else they aren't "okay." But, if you do not deal with nonperformers, your good people will suffer. Wal-Mart's managers aren't hesitant to deal with performance issues head on and you shouldn't be either.

In any work group, all of the employees are cognizant of how they are performing in relation to others. If you don't deal directly with nonperformance, you will create self-inflicted work group morale problems. You have to send the message to your good performers that doing a good job around here is important. You also have to send the opposite message to the nonperformers that failure to perform is not okay and will lead to disciplinary action. Make a point of recognizing those who consistently do a good job, and don't hesitate to communicate your disapproval to those who aren't performing.

Performance feedback is a powerful motivator and it's also a form of recognition. A *Fortune 500* company CEO once said, "If you want to recognize someone do it publicly; if you want to give them performance feedback do it privately." The message is *catch employees doing things right*! Accentuate the positive behavior of individuals or your team publicly and eliminate negative behavior privately, behind closed doors. Like Mr. Sam, be a fact-finder not a fault-finder. We all spend an inordinate amount of time, energy, and effort on the employees who are sucking the vitality out of the organization, rather than spending time with the top performers who are working with us to create team synergy. My opinion is that you should spend more time on the top-performing 90 percent of your work group and either upgrade or cut your losses on the lower 10 percent.

As you begin to catch people doing things right, you will also simultaneously need to continue to deal with the nonperformers. Over time, you will want to quietly eliminate the poor performers by providing them with feedback, which may move their performance up, or you'll have to move them out of the organization. By systematically dealing with your lowest performers and replacing them with employees with higher potential, you will upgrade the performance of your entire team.

Imagine how your job would improve if you had a team of positive-performing employees, in every job, trying to help you hit your performance goals every day! Yes, that is possible and yes, that is within the scope of your responsibilities to accomplish, now! The act of balancing the recognition of good performers and dealing with nonperformers creates equilibrium in the work group and sends employees the message that all is right with the world.

This harmony, which you as a leader are responsible for creating, makes your job of achieving performance standards much easier than it would be otherwise. In plain and simple language, when you hold people accountable to standards, you are being a good leader. That's the "Sam Walton way!"

Mr. Sam believed if you come through for others, show them you care, and recognize their efforts, they will come through for you. Sam Walton's legion of loyal managers and associates love and respect him to this day He shunned personal recognition throughout his life, but his loyal followers have recognized his leadership posthumously by adopting his beliefs as their own and continuing to commit themselves to helping him achieve his dream of making Wal-Mart the best retailer in the world.

CELEBRATE Your Own and Other's Accomplishments

Sam Walton believed in having fun
and celebrating all kinds of milestones
like the successful achievement of a goal,
a birthday, or the birth of a child!

A Wal-Mart executive, who had previously worked for one of Sam Walton's competitors back in the early days of Wal-Mart, told the story of the day he attended one of Mr. Sam's original new store openings. He said it was one of the worst new store openings he had ever seen! It was an unusually hot, Midwest summer day; well over 100° with high humidity and no wind. To begin with, picture in your mind a corral set up right in front of the store filled with donkeys. Mr. Sam had advertised free donkey rides as a way to attract families with children to come shop at the store. Displayed next to the donkey corral was the biggest display of watermelons you'll ever see, which he had stacked directly on the asphalt parking lot. When the sun came up, and the day wore on, that asphalt got so hot you could have fried eggs on it! With all that heat and all that sun, those watermelons sitting directly on the asphalt got so hot they began to pop and the juice of those watermelons flowed across the parking lot. Now picture those donkeys, doing what donkeys do, and that too was mixed with the watermelon juice. All those families had to slog through that awful concoction and in the process carried a lot of it into the store on the bottom of their shoes. The floors inside the store were a filthy mess and the place smelled terrible. It was the worst new store opening this executive had ever seen.

This Sam Walton story has become part of the folklore of the company, representing its humble roots. It provides an excellent illustration of how far Mr. Sam was willing to go to differentiate his business and create a fun environment for his associates and his customers. This is an example of Mr. Sam's sixth success secret for achieving remarkable results: *"CELEBRATE your own and other's accomplishments."* He didn't believe company leaders and associates should take themselves too seriously. One way to do just that was to have a sense of humor and to try to have fun. He wanted his stores to always be an enjoyable experience for his customers. His management team was encouraged to loosen up and be enthusiastic so that the associates around them would, too. In the early days of Wal-Mart, Sam Walton's competitors didn't take him seriously, and I think it was because of the widely known stunts he pulled and his fun antics.

Mr. Sam believed in breaking the boredom by trying to make things fun and exciting. That's one of the reasons he created the famous Wal-Mart cheer. He picked up the idea on a trip to a tennis ball factory in Korea. Mr. Sam's Wal-Mart cheer goes like this: "Give me a W! Give me an A! Give me an L! Give me a Squiggly! Give me an M! Give me an A! Give me an R! Give me a T! What's that spell? Wal-Mart! Whose Wal-Mart is it? My Wal-Mart! Who's number one? The customer...always!" Sam Walton enthusiastically led and performed the Wal-Mart cheer whenever he visited a store or a distribution center. He viewed the cheer as a way of differentiating everybody on the Wal-Mart team from everybody else.

Because the stores are 24/7/365, distribution center managers and company store managers conduct Wal-Mart cheers across three shifts. With all associates in plain view of customers, company managers sometimes hold meetings near the cash registers at the front of the store, where they conduct a Wal-Mart cheer for all to hear and see. One store manager told me, "I have had customers come into the store with a frown on their face and once they'd see us doing the cheer, they'd start laughing and walk over and actually join in and participate in the Wal-Mart cheer with the associates." I know the first time I experienced a Wal-Mart cheer I was shocked and awed by the fanatical enthusiasm with which the associates participated. I can't even imagine what that same experience does to a customer walking in the front door of the store when faced with a Wal-Mart cheer being executed at a fever pitch!

The enthusiasm, loyalty, and out-and-out fanaticism of Wal-Mart's people, both managers and hourly paid associates, has led some outside observers to accuse the company of operating some kind of cult. One of Webster's definitions of a cult is "great devotion to a person, idea or thing." Well if you use that definition, Mr. Sam's associates truly are loyal disciples who have *great devotion* to his *idea,* which is everyday low prices and good customer service. Another way to look at Wal-Mart's culture is an unending devotion and focus on the customer. Mr. Sam was devoted to those customers, and his beloved army of associates is devoted to those customers as well. If a cult in a business context is a group of motivated people all working enthusiastically toward serving the needs of its customers, than call it what you will. I believe the real cult at Wal-Mart is the 130 million customers per week who make the pilgrimage to its stores in a low-priced-product-induced trance to fill their shopping carts to overflowing with too-good-to-be-true bargains! The *thing* that motivates this customer cult's *great devotion* is their discount store of choice, Wal-Mart.

Wal-Mart's associates take ownership of the business and enthusiastically serve the customers because they are business owners. Many of the company's associates buy stock through Wal-Mart's associate stock purchase plan and many, including truck drivers, distribution center employees, and store associates, have became millionaires as a result. The loyalty of Wal-Mart's associates is a result of the partnership Mr. Sam created with them from the very beginning. The loyalty of his associates was not simply a result of making lots of money through owning company stock and profit sharing. We have all heard stories of rich people who are miserable in life. Mr. Sam was committed to his team of associates and he cared about them. In turn, his associates loved and respected him as their leader. They still remember him to this day with respect because of the way he treated people. It was his loyalty to them and how he treated them that engendered strong loyalty in return.

Sam Walton was one part preacher like Billy Graham, one part ringmaster like P.T. Barnum, and one part comedian like Bob Hope. He was a charismatic leader with a sense of humor who enjoyed preaching his philosophies to his disciples every chance he had. He also truly enjoyed being out on center stage like a ring-master at a shareholders meetings or at a Saturday morning meeting, hawking his wares and giving his loyal followers direction. You never quite knew what Mr. Sam would talk about, but you knew whatever he said would be inspirational and that it would be peppered with humor most of which was directed at himself or at one of the members of his executive leadership team.

Mr. Sam's preaching, comedy, and ever-changing retail circus atmosphere were designed to shock the systems of his associates and his customers. By shocking their systems, he created powerful emotional connections with people; I've heard this referred to as *creating a significant emotional event.* When this happens, there is a much higher retention rate of whatever the message is by those receiving it. By providing the unexpected and creating a fun and memorable atmosphere, Wal-Mart makes its customers want to come back again and again to experience those same feelings. The same was true for Mr. Sam's associates, who were unusually loyal to him, many willing to forgo other opportunities in order to stay at Wal-Mart to work around Mr. Sam. They liked him so much and held him in such high regard that he was often asked by his own associates for his autograph or to have their picture taken with him!

I think the reason Mr. Sam took the approach he did to moti-vating people was partly based of the realities facing most suc-cessful entrepreneurs. As a company gets larger and larger, it becomes more and more difficult for its leader to get and hold the attention of the people working there. A quote from Harry Truman about Dwight Eisenhower captures this challenge of leadership very well: "Poor Ike; when he was a general, he gave an order and it was carried out. Now, he's going to sit in that Presidential office and give an order and nothing will happen." What Truman was saying is that unlike the military, managers and employees in organizations today do not or may not execute on command. That's the same challenge Sam Walton faced as his company grew larger and larger. He figured out that his associates would be much more likely to execute if he treated them with respect, asked for their help, listened to their concerns, and got them involved in establishing the organization's mission, objectives, and strategies. He also realized that the work was easier to perform if people had fun while doing it. I believe Sam Walton's charismatic leadership was part of who he was and as Wal-Mart grew larger and larger, his style of leadership was pivotal to the success of the company. You might say he was the right man, in the right place, at the right time.

Company managers are encouraged and expected to continuously come up with ways to break the boredom and have fun at work. Clearly, there is method to their madness. Happy and positive employees lead to happy customers and happy customers, lead to larger purchases and return customers. The opposite is also true. Negative or hostile employees with bad attitudes negatively impact customers and may even drive customers away, forever. Sam Walton realized the key to his success was in courting his customers to return again and again. Knowing customers have an endless array of choices on which they can spend their money, he expected his store managers to do everything they possibly could to make Wal-Mart the friendliest store out there. By achieving this goal, customers would make Wal-Mart their one-stop shopping destination of choice each and every week of the year.

If you think about it, most of us have had the experience of trying to do business with a company whose employees are clearly unhappy with their jobs. That unhappiness is reflected in the way they handle customers. I, for one, won't spend my money at a company that doesn't appreciate my business, and I'd be willing to bet you won't either. That's why Mr. Sam worked so hard to create a friendly, fun, and welcoming environment for his customers, but he knew that kind of positive atmosphere is a result of happy associates. Here's how one of Wal-Mart's store managers described how he celebrated associate successes and created a positive shopping atmosphere for customers in his store:

> Have fun; when you set a goal and when you reach your goal, have a party and celebrate it! Cheer people on like they do a baseball team or a football team. People want to be encouraged. People want to be told that they did a good job there, thank you. I think it is very important to tell my management team every night, "thank you," you did a good job today. It's important when I see them doing a good job, coaching the associates, to tell them that I notice. As a leader, you have to encourage people and cheer them on to do their best. We use customer service awards, great job pins for receiving customer compliments, there is a customer choice award, and the district managers even recognize associates or managers with lapel pins for doing a good job at taking care of the customers. We believe in appreciating people for what they do.

The motivational approach used at Wal-Mart is designed to modify and focus the behavior of its associates to achieve sale and service goals, and it is obviously working. Many of Wal-Mart's customers shop its stores each week, most returning again and again. Some drive considerable distances, passing competitors stores along the way in favor of spending their hard-earned dollars at the friendliest store around with the lowest prices. Wal-Mart's "one-two punch" of great service and low prices has a devastating impact on its competition while engendering cult-like loyalty from its customers. In the process the company has been transported to the top of the *Fortune* 500 list. It is now the biggest and most successful company in the world and growing.

Even though the approach used to celebrate its successes may be perceived as a little hokey by others, Wal-Mart's associates enjoy and appreciate the efforts of their company leaders to care enough to try to break the boredom and make coming to work an enjoyable experience. So let's talk about the ways and means of motivating people by celebrating successes at Wal-Mart, the theory behind it, and how Sam Walton did it sincerely and effectively.

Did you ever hear that story about the manager who was asked the employee the question, "What's the difference between ignorance and apathy?" To which the employee responded, "I don't know and I don't care!" This story provides a nice lead into how Wal-Mart approaches motivating people to achieve the goals of the company. The definition of ignorance is *not knowing,* and the definition of apathy is *not caring.* When managers don't communicate, employees experience that feeling of ignorance by not knowing what is going on. Interestingly enough, employees also experience apathy as a result of a manager who doesn't care enough to communicate with them. Managers who intentionally or unintentionally don't communicate thrust employees into a "veil of darkness" which is both stressful and demotivating. The result is higher turnover of employees, poor service, and lower sales.

Can organizational leaders truly motivate employees? The correct answer is that true motivation has to come from within the individual. Leaders have to create a positive climate or environment within which employees become self-motivated. When that happens, ordinary people can accomplish extraordinary things. Unfortunately, poor leaders can create a demotivating climate or environment, which leads to poor morale and low productivity.

Wal-Mart, like every other company, has pockets of negativity that when analyzed can be attributed to poor leadership. In my own experience, when I've found a systemic issue of poor morale and bad attitudes in a company or work group, I can almost always accurately attribute it to a poor leader. Until and unless an organization with poor morale implements positive changes in the way it approaches its own people, the poor morale won't change. Some organizations seem to take the position that the change necessary needs to occur in the employees themselves by embracing the philosophy that "the floggings will continue until morale improves." That's the wrong way to look at employee motivation. I have never found in my own experience a large group of bad employees. I have often found a group of employees who exhibit poor morale as a result of poor leadership. The creation of a positive culture starts at the top, and it happens as a result of leaders who sincerely care about people; that's how Sam Walton was so successful in his dealings with his associates.

Mr. Sam would tell you that the single best tool you have in your management tool kit for creating a positive employee relations climate is the use of positive recognition. That's why Wal-Mart and Sam Walton believe in celebrating successes. There are, however, significant differences in how much recognition each individual actually wants or desires. Some people find being recognized privately better, whereas others thrive on being recognized publicly. You have to know your people to understand their individual recognition hot buttons.

In the old days a boot to the butt was what they called motivation. They used the paycheck itself as a weapon. "Do the job or else," was the implied message. "It's my way or the highway" was the quote the old timers used to use. People are too smart these days to put up with that kind of treatment. Today there are lots of companies competing for the same pool of talented people in the workforce. If you want to get your share of great people, you have to give them a reason to work for you.

Mr. Sam believed it started with helping associates find meaning and purpose in their work. By helping them understand the company, their job, and their career paths, he helped them see the bigger picture. They saw how their work related to that of the rest of the team and through that process saw the end results of their efforts.

Mr. Sam believed that every single one of his associates really wanted to do a good job, and they wanted to be part of something special and to make a difference. Herein lies your opportunity to recognize your people and in the process, "with nothing up your sleeves," improve performance of individuals and your entire work group. There is a direct relationship between recognizing employees and increased productivity. This is because people who feel good about themselves feel better about their jobs, and are more motivated to increase productivity. One of the store managers who worked with Sam Walton told me how he recognized the associates in his store, which directly impacted his store's performance:

> The big successes like a good inventory you might do a cookout for the associates out behind the store for every shift. It's kind of interesting to get out behind the store at midnight and grill steaks for the third shift, but they are as important as everybody else. You might recognize individuals at morning meetings or take a group of individuals to lunch, again across

all three shifts. You can recognize people in big ways and in small ways and a lot of times that really depends on knowing the individual and what motivates them. Some people are really embarrassed and uncomfortable being recognized in a big group, but if you as a store manager can get the district manager to go over and speak to them one on one, sometimes that means more than all the accolades in the world. In the store, monthly we did birthday cakes. VPI (volume producing item) winners were recognized every month in store meetings and also their pictures were put up on the wall, recognizing what they did and what were their sales and profit volume. The sales and profit numbers for the store were posted every month on big charts right by the time clock for everybody to see and be a part of.

There are so many ways that Wal-Mart demonstrates its appreciation for its associates. It starts with a thorough orientation of its newly hired associates and then continues as the company provides training. Some of that training is conducted by more senior associates, who may also act as a mentor to new people. The company recognizes good performers by offering them new job responsibilities and more challenging work. Cross-training assignments may even provide associates with promotional opportunities to higher-level jobs.

Wal-Mart's managers are taught to praise associates for a job well done. Mr. Sam wanted his managers to appreciate everything the associates did for the company. That's because Wal-Mart has a recognition culture where catching people doing things right is a daily occurrence. He believed in encouraging people with a good old-fashioned pat on the back. He believed there was no better way to let people know you appreciated them than to listen to them and to then respond to their concerns. He also understood the value of asking their opinions. Often when Mr. Sam talked with associates, he'd talk in terms of their interests. He'd talk about their families or hobbies or what was of interest to them. Sam Walton was even known for sending handwritten notes of appreciation to associates and to customers.

A former Wal-Mart Store manager told me this story about Mr. Sam:

> I met Sam Walton many times. I still have two handwritten letters that he wrote to me. Keep in mind, this is the richest man in America. He could have dictated a letter to his secretary and she could have rubber stamped it. Once he met you he always remembered you. He walked up to me, shook my hand, and said that it was good to talk to me when we didn't have a crisis. He could remember stuff about people—it was just unreal. He'd come in the store and see people he'd talk to once a year or every year and a half, when the company was still small enough that he could do that. He said to a female associate, "the last time I was here your husband was in the hospital; is he okay?" How did he remember all these people? He was very personable and able to communicate with every single hourly associate no matter what their status was, no matter what their position was, or how much money they made; it really didn't matter. When the company lost Sam Walton they lost someone really special.

He was one of those rare people you meet in life who never met a stranger.

Mr. Sam believed in using common courtesies in his dealings with people. He used people's names when he spoke to them, and he respectfully used terms like *please* and *thank you*. Simple things were important to him like making eye contact with people and saying good morning as he passed them in the hallway. One of Mr. Sam's store managers described him as follows: "He was people oriented. He was just a top notch 'people person.' He'd come in and even if you had never met him before in your life, he made you feel like you had known him forever." It was he who would more often than not initiate a conversation to break the ice with someone who might otherwise be intimidated when first meeting him.

Here are some tips you can use to provide quality recognition the Wal-Mart way. Try to time the recognition so that it is given as soon as possible following the desired behavior. When you publicly recognize one or more of your employees, it helps establish a benchmark for all the others to follow. The key to recognition and praise is that it must be sincere; otherwise it loses its value as a motivational tool. Because it's free, there is no restriction on the amount sincere recognition that can be used by any leader. Once recognition leads to better results, managers have a tendency to use it again in the future, because of its proven value. Leaders at Wal-Mart and in your organization must earn the right to use recognition as a performance motivator by first gaining the trust and respect of the employees in the work group; only than will sincere recognition be effective.

One of Wal-Mart's store managers told me how he planned success celebrations into his weekly management routine, "We have staff meetings every Friday, and at those meetings we celebrate associates' birthdays. Those departments with current sales that exceeded last year's sales were recognized as well by giving them awards or lapel pins to recognize them for the great job they had done." As in this example, it is a good idea to plan celebrations into your work routine so that they happen regularly. Ideally, some kind of recognition activity should be occurring throughout the year.

Managers were trained to post notes from customers on bulletin boards for everyone to see. They would also review those notes at one of the daily meetings held with associates. Stellar performances of individuals and entire departments were also showcased at those daily meetings as a form of public recognition.

In every organization there are plenty of opportunities every day to catch employees doing things right. The following is a list, which is not all-inclusive, of several inexpensive ideas for positive individual and group celebrations and recognition:

- Attendance luncheons
- Birthday celebrations
- Years of service awards
- Certificates/plaques/ pins
- Peer recognition
- Suggestion boxes
- Letters to the employee's home

- Productivity improvement awards
- Customer recognition of employees
- Employee of the month
- Sales/service/expense commenda- tions
- Pot luck lunches or donut day
- Company picnics
- Pizza parties recognizing an achievement

These kinds of nonmonetary award ideas can be developed into an action plan at your company or in your work group with minor effort. Wal-Mart doesn't strive for perfection and neither should you; remember it's hard to "screw up" when you are sincere about providing recognition! If you don't currently have a celebration program, you are better off keeping it simple. Don't attempt to implement all kinds of disjointed and confusing activities simultaneously. Put one recognition activity in place, get it running properly, and then work on another. Eventually, you will have a calendar of recognition activities occurring year round.

The benefits you'll gain for the work you put in to this can be phenomenal. People who previously didn't seem to care become responsive. You may even achieve new levels of performance that in the past didn't seem possible. There are some key questions to ask yourself:

- Are you celebrating anniversaries and birthdays in your work group?

- Do you celebrate when employees achieve performance goals?
- Are employees thanked for a job well done?
- Is employee performance reviewed periodically?
- Are sales, service, and safety success stories celebrated?
- Is excellent attendance recognized?
- Do you celebrate individual as well as team achievements?

How did you answer these questions? Are you already celebrating the contributions of your employees or do you need to start? I challenge you to implement one or more of these simple programs in your organization, now! I think you'll find there is little doubt that it works. Sam Walton learned this important lesson and you should, too: Behavior that gets rewarded has a tendency to be repeated. Nonmonetary awards or rewards can have a dramatic positive impact on morale, productivity, safety, service, attendance, and teamwork.

There is no better way to create excitement around company goals than through challenging employees with individual or team-based contests. The reward for achievement could be as simple as an award certificate or a free lunch. Sam Walton really liked nonmonetary recognition because it had high impact and no cost. For this reason, Mr. Sam liked managers to set up contests and create competition within each of his stores. Posting the goals of the contest and then personally updating the results daily helps maintain focus and enthusiasm for achieving the desired goal. Publicly recognizing those who hit the target demonstrates the importance of performance to your work group.

A Wal-Mart store manager, who had met Sam Walton many times, told me how he used Mr. Sam's ideas when he held contests and celebrated success in his store:

> I worked for Wal-Mart for 27 years. I have taken a pie in the
> face when I lost a contest. I've swapped jobs with people. I've

dressed up in a clown costume and then stood at the door greeting customers; I might be the greeter for 2 or 3 hours. When I was an assistant manager, I challenged the other assistant manager to a contest and the loser had to dress up in a costume for a day. I've seen management shave their heads when a goal is achieved. I've taken groups of associates out to lunch because they've reached goals. We'd give out customer service awards and great job pins when someone receives a customer compliment. There's even a customer choice award for outstanding service. We believe in celebrating the successes of people by showing them we appreciate what they do.

Mr. Sam led by example by creating his own crazy contests. Back in the early 1980s, he promised that if the company had a pretax profit of 8 percent or higher that year, he would do the hula, in a grass skirt, on Wall Street. The company associates kept their part of the bargain and he kept his. He donned a grass skirt and accompanied by real hula dancers, ukulele players, and the press corps, Sam Walton did the hula on Wall Street as promised. This story has become part of the folklore of the company and is used to illustrate how far Wal-Mart's leaders are willing to go to create excitement and have fun while celebrating the achievement of company goals.

If Sam Walton, the CEO of the world's most successful company, believed in using contests, celebrations, and recognition to drive his business, there are obviously some pretty terrific benefits to doing so. I can assure you that like everything else Wal-Mart does, the use of fun celebration activities has a bottom-line impact. Some of the cultural benefits include better morale, lower stress, enhanced training, uniform standards, reduced turnover, better teamwork, and higher productivity. The combination of well-run contests, planned celebrations, and targeted recognition activities provides a Swiss Army Knife–like assortment of tools Wal-Mart's leaders can use to improve and enhance their business.

How did Mr. Sam use contests, celebrations, and recognition to drive his business forward? He did it by starting with the end in mind. If he wanted to address a problem with his associates regarding better customer service, he'd develop a contest around service. If he wanted to teach better merchandising skills, he'd create a competition around building the best merchandising display. If lowering expenses was a concern, he'd set up a contest to see which departments could meet or lower their expense budgets. By getting people involved in doing an activity to improve an area of the operation, he was teaching everyone his standards. Instead of lecturing associates on how to do something or browbeating them to do it, he designed activities that actually made learning and achieving a fun experience for everyone.

Celebrating success is another one of Sam Walton's cultural success secrets. He figured out a way years ago to get all of his people to focus on the same activities and to do it the Wal-Mart way. His culture is the glue that holds Wal-Mart's stores and distribution centers together to this day. His ability to mobilize his army of associates to focus on improving specific areas of the business using contests, celebrations, and recognition created a competitive advantage for him in the marketplace. He always said that competitors could duplicate his stores, his products, and his merchandising, but the one thing they couldn't replicate was the wonderful Wal-Mart culture!

LISTEN to Others and Learn from Their Ideas

Mr. Sam believed in listening to the people
who are closest to the customer
because they understood better than
anyone else what the customers
really want and need.

◄●►

S am Walton acknowledged that the single most important thing that he did for Wal-Mart was his visits to his own stores. He would rather be out with the folks doing the real work of retail than sit around in meetings in the home office. He really felt he could help the stores by visiting them; if something needed fixing, he could help them fix it. He enjoyed talking with and listening to the associates on those visits. I remember trying to schedule him to lead a panel discussion on a live satellite broadcast going to colleges across America, weeks in advance, and he refused to give me a firm commitment because he said he might decide to jump in his airplane and fly out to a store at the last minute. That's how much he enjoyed his visits with the associates in the stores. The truth be told, it was the one thing he enjoyed more in business than anything else. While out in the stores, he was on a very specific mission. His goal was to gain firsthand competitive intelligence about his competitor's stores, talk to and learn from some of his own customers, and most important of all spend time talking with his own associates.

Mr. Sam's seventh success secret for achieving remarkable results is *"LISTEN to others and learn from their ideas."* He believed that everyone who works for a company has good ideas they are willing to share if company leaders will take the time to ask for them. The trick, he said, was in figuring out how to get people talking. He did it by wandering around his stores, asking the associates questions, and then actively listening to their responses. He truly believed that the people closest to the customer were the ones who really had a handle on what customers were thinking and feeling about his stores. If he were to give others specific advice, it would be to out what the employees who are closest to your customers know and use that information to improve your organization.

Because Mr. Sam believed the most important employees at Wal-Mart were the associates in contact with the customer, he empowered them to serve the customer. As his business partners, he gave them the responsibility and authority to do their jobs; then he asked them for their best ideas and used them to improve the business. He believed that leaders needed to serve those in the organization who worked *with* them. He felt that if you wanted to build any kind of lasting relationship with the associates, you had to become a master at communicating with them and listening to them. His listening formula is the same formula you should use in your organization: Listen to your managers, your employees, and your customers and gather their ideas and implement them. It is as simple as that!

The vision of Sam Walton poised on one knee within a circle of associates sitting on the floor around him gives you a picture of how important associate two-way communication was to him. He repeated this exercise in every store he visited, pulling the associates together in the front of the store or in the break room. Sometimes he held these impromptu meetings in full view of the customers who were shopping in the store. He talked and he listened. He let people know how much he appreciated their efforts and results. His genuine concern for people was legendary. Here's an insight from one of his early store managers:

> When Mr. Sam came into the stores, he didn't come into the stores to visit the store managers, he came to visit with the department managers and associates. Department managers in a Wal-Mart are all hourly paid associates, and those were the people he would start talking with when he visited a store. He'd get them in the break room or sitting on the floor or standing around in the soft-lines area because he was inter-

ested in talking with them and hearing about what was going
on. He wanted to know what kinds of ideas they had and
what was going right and what was going wrong. He had such
a charisma about him that people would just tell him everything. He had a very good memory and which might be
because he was a Captain in army intelligence. With his military background and his memory, especially of people and
places, he would never forget someone after having met them
and he might even recall a specific discussion he had with
them about their family.

Sam Walton believed that the respectful treatment of his associates and the maintenance of a positive associate relations culture
went hand-in-hand with the success of a work group, department,
manufacturing facility, store, distribution center, or a company. He
was so committed to this belief that when he spoke with groups
of Wal-Mart's executives, managers, and supervisors, he often
proclaimed, "If you take care of your people, your people will
take care of the customers, and the business will take care of
itself." Clearly, he realized he couldn't accomplish the massive task
of listening and responding to the needs of his associates through
his own efforts alone. Through his own example he showed his
entire leadership team specific techniques they could use to understand the needs of the associates, and he taught them various ways
they could prove to people how much they cared. By using those
same skills, Sam Walton received undying loyalty and enthusiastic
teamwork from his thousands of associate business partners.

Sam Walton's managers and associates, in every department,
worked together as a team to accomplish company goals. That same
level of cooperation existed within and between departments. At
Wal-Mart, everyone worked together enthusiastically to accomplish
the goals of the company. Sam Walton valued team success more

highly than individual success and for this reason recognition-seeking egotistical prima donnas don't do well at the world's largest retailer.

There is one agenda at Wal-Mart, and that is the company agenda. Departmental or functional agendas are downplayed or they don't exist! Everyone in every department bends over backward to help one another. At Wal-Mart, they call this practice *internal customer service*. When I worked there, the esprit de corps and cooperation I experienced between people and departments reminded me of the battle cry of the Three Musketeers: "It's all for one and one for all!"

How did Sam Walton get that level of loyalty, cooperation, and teamwork? I can tell you it started with the top executives at Wal-Mart, who embrace a leadership philosophy called *servant leadership*. Servant leadership in an organizational context is defined as organizational leaders putting the needs of the employees reporting to them first. Said another way, leaders need to serve the needs of employees who report to them first, thereby gaining their respect and trust and by doing so the servant leader earns the right to lead the team. In practice at Wal-Mart, managers never ask the associates to do anything they haven't already proven through their actions that they are willing to do personally. Sam Walton's servant leaders at Wal-Mart actively listen to the associates and responded to their needs. By using servant leadership with sincerity, Sam Walton discovered a powerful way to teach company leaders to motivate individuals and teams.

Mr. Sam believed in leading by example by being a servant leader. He defined a true servant leader as someone who serves the people who report to him or her first and then secondarily as the associates begin to respect their supervisor they may choose to follow. He never asked anyone to do anything he had not already proven he was willing to do himself. Using this approach, he was able to foster extremely positive associate relations. He believed in serving the needs of people first by helping them. Mr. Sam's brand of servant leadership came from the heart. Leaders either sincerely care about people or they don't. If they do care, great morale, camaraderie, and motivation are the end result. Insincere or half-hearted efforts on the part of a manager will be taken as such, causing morale and performance of employees to deteriorate. To be a true servant leader the Wal-Mart way requires company leaders to be fully immersed in the business and listen to the concerns and ideas of employees. The benefit of servant leadership to Wal-Mart is the creation of team synergy. When that happens, the collective effort of teams of motivated associates exceeds the actual sum of the efforts of the individual members.

Sam Walton believed employees don't really care what their manager or supervisor knows until that manager or supervisor shows the employees how much he or she cares about them. By taking this approach, Sam Walton's managers and supervisors established trusting, caring relationships with their associates that over time lead to cooperation and teamwork. At Wal-Mart a servant leader with a team of motivated associates working together enthusiastically has the ability to meet and even exceed the goals of the organization.

Servant leadership has a positive bottom-line impact at Wal-Mart to this day. I asked one of the store managers how the company trains its managers to be servant leaders. I was told it isn't as much a trained behavior as it is a learned behavior. The culture demands its leaders care about people, and anything less is unacceptable. One of the quickest ways to fail at Wal-Mart is for a leader to lack the ability to relate to people and create team synergy. Motivated people are the key to achieving the difficult goals of the company; without the support of the associates, a manager is destined to fail.

How does Wal-Mart motivate people to the lofty levels of team synergy? It's accomplished by putting the emotional needs of people first. The company starts by hiring managers who are down to earth. The managers I have met are unpretentious, people-oriented individuals. It's no secret that they like working with and being around the associates. This caring attitude comes across loud and clear, and the associates can sense the sincerity of company leaders. They listen, respond to concerns, and use associate ideas and they hold daily meetings to keep the associates informed. The store managers, distribution center managers, and fleet management team at Wal-Mart and Sam's Club see the powerful impact of Sam Walton's philosophies firsthand. One of the managers shared this insight with me:

> Mr. Sam was so genuine about his friendliness. No matter whom he dealt with, whether it was hourly associates, vendors, or manufacturers, it had to be a win-win situation. He believed if you wanted to be successful, you had to have that philosophy. He learned a long time ago that as you are going up the success ladder, if you stepped on people, it would eventually lead to your demise. It is very important for that reason to share your success.

Mr. Sam's grand design for motivating Wal-Mart's throng of associates was developed around a variety of strategies and tactics with the purpose of garnering loyalty and above-average performance from his associates. His holistic approach to motivation included a company communications program, proactive associate relations, a focused training program in job-specific technical skills, and development of the most important personal skills. His goal was to create an environment of openness, cooperation, teamwork, and motivation. Using his beliefs about servant leadership as the foundation, he taught his management disciples the importance of having and using strong people skills to foster a positive work environment. The ultimate goal of his motivational strategy was the creation of the most important piece of the productivity puzzle, team synergy.

Here's why it is important to communicate with and listen to associates. Each store or distribution center at Wal-Mart operates like a stand-alone company. The store manager or distribution center manager is responsible for everything inside those four walls. The associates who work for the company typically don't know anything about the company except what goes on inside their own store or distribution center. Their initial orientation, training, company meetings, newsletters, bulletin boards, peer level socialization, interaction with managers, company rituals, folklore, company policies, and procedures all build the cultural foundation upon which team synergy is created. It isn't any one thing that is representative of the Sam Walton or Wal-Mart way. The company, with all of its efforts to simplify everything else, weaves a complex cultural web around its managers and associates. This intricate cultural web has turned Wal-Mart's culture into an impenetrable fortress that has perplexed competitors. Mr. Sam always said, "Everything else Wal-Mart does is visible for competitors to observe and replicate, but they can't duplicate our unique Wal-Mart culture."

Mr. Sam believed that everyone had knowledge from which he could learn. I listened to him when he talked to someone he had never spoken with before. The wealthiest man in the world would ask open-ended questions and then quietly listen to others talk about the keys to their success. Most of the time, he would take notes that he would refer to and apply later. He used this same approach when dealing with associates, suppliers, or customers. Imagine what individuals could have learned from him if they were able to get him to talk more and they could listen to his ideas! His patient listening skills contributed to his success as much as his ability to sell his own ideas. As a life-long learner, he was committed to constantly increasing his own knowledge. He used new information that he received from listening to others to improve every aspect of Wal-Mart. With his legal pad and pen in hand, he traveled the world in search of new ideas and a better way. He often said there wasn't a day that went by that he didn't learn something new that he could later use. He was almost child-like in his wanderlust for learning.

Sam Walton once said, "It is amazing what a team of selfless people can accomplish if nobody is worried about who is going to get the credit in the end." This is the idea behind gathering ideas from everyone at Wal-Mart. Mr. Sam knew that good ideas were everywhere; he just had to find them. He openly solicited input from every associate; they responded with lots of small and even some big solutions to business problems. This tradition continues in the company to this day. Here's how a store manager describes it:

> Because of the way associates are empowered to take owner-
> ship, there are ideas coming up every single day. Each associ-
> ate treats the business like as her or his own; the associate was
> always looking for some way to make a mark on it. The ideas
> bubbled up all the time and Wal-Mart made such a huge deal
> out of celebrating those ideas which were successes. You still
> hear that the people greeter at the front door of Wal-Mart
> came from an idea from one store down in Louisiana; Mr. Sam
> saw it and loved it. Now every store in the world is doing it;

other retailers are doing it too. That story has been told again and again and is now part of company folklore. It's part of Wal-Mart's philosophy of celebrating successes. There are always ideas coming up in the stores that the associates implement and could possibly spread across departments; occasionally ideas reached the district level, maybe even the region would adopt them.

Sam Walton viewed the discovery of good ideas as he would the discovery of buried treasure. In a way, that's exactly what he'd found. Ideas are free and if the problem they solve is business related, the savings can impact the bottom line. A good idea that saves time reduces payroll hours. A method for improving the merchandising of products can increase sales. The ideas needed in a Wal-Mart store are endless for empowered associates, thinking like business owners, to come up with important solutions to real problems.

As servant leaders the company's managers never ask associates to do anything they haven't already proven through their actions that they are personally willing to do themselves. It's not unusual for a manager to be seen collecting shopping carts in the parking lot, cleaning up a spill, interacting with customers, or greeting customers at the entrance to the store. The combination of all of Mr. Sam's employee-centered activities created a caring and trusting environment within which teamwork flourished. Sam Walton figured out that the path to synergy begins with servant leadership—by first showing you care about associates, listening and responding to their concerns, and creating trust. Caring and trust are the prerequisites for real teamwork, and the combination leads to team synergy. Empowering individuals, coupled with the synergy of teams to control costs, serves the customers, develops better ways of doing things, and leads to magical accomplishments within individual stores and distribution centers around the world. The idea for creating a team of motivated associates at Wal-Mart can be boiled down to servant leaders working together with empowered people to achieve team synergy.

At Wal-Mart, company leaders are held accountable for the way they treat people and build loyalty. There are several methods or tools used at Wal-Mart for tracking for keeping track of how the associates are feeling about the company and the leadership team closest to them. These are the tools Sam Walton put in place for communicating with and listening to his associates:

- One-on-one meetings
- Grass-roots opinion surveys
- Safety
- Attendance policy
- Performance coaching
- Open-door policy
- Daily meetings
- Exit interviews
- Retention and turnover
- SMART evaluations

All of these tools are designed to contribute to Sam Walton's management goal of listening to the associates, showing management cares and responding to associate concerns. Here is a review of each of these from a Wal-Mart perspective.

One-on-one meetings between managers and associates are designed to allow two-way communications. These meetings may take place in the break room, snack bar, manager's office, warehouse, or out on the sales floor. One-on-one meetings can be planned but are typically unplanned with the manager simply stopping to talk with associates with whom he or she comes in contact. These brief meetings provide the manager and the associate with an opportunity to get to know one another on a more personal and familiar level. These brief encounters provide the associates with ample opportunities to share their concerns or to suggest a new idea. From a management viewpoint, spending time with associates provides a chance to see what everyone is thinking and feeling; it is an excellent way to get a sense for overall morale.

One of the things that facilitated communication at Wal-Mart was the informality of the place. Everyone, including the executives at the home office, was easy to see and meet with, and you didn't necessarily have to have an appointment to stop by to talk with them. An associate from Wal-Mart's stores, who later became a merchandise buyer for the company, shared this story with me:

> In all of my dealings with Mr. Sam, he was always accessible. They had what was called "executive row" at the corporate offices and I remember when I was taking a class one week at the corporate offices, I wanted to get a shirt signed by Sam Walton while I was there, so I walked over to executive row. The whole group of executives had offices you could walk right up to; they were so accessible and you could walk right into the executive's offices. Unfortunately Mr. Sam wasn't there at the time because he was out visiting stores. His executive assistant said she would take care of getting the autograph for me later. The next day she walked into the classroom and handed me my shirt which had been signed by Mr. Sam. Everyone attending that class was ogling that shirt.

Sam Walton and the executives he had working for him were unpretentious individuals who valued people and believed in good communication. To this day, the openness and accessibility of the executives at Wal-Mart to meet and speak with the associates is truly extraordinary.

Grass-roots associate opinion surveys are conducted once a year in the stores, distribution centers, and home office. The survey is designed to collect associate opinions on a variety of work-related topics and once the data are compiled, local managers meet with groups of associates to discuss the results. The 23 questions used in the survey are focused in two major areas: people skills and work processes. The key leadership competencies evaluated in the survey under people skills are communication, developing others, motivating others, customer focus, and listening. The work processes key competencies include continuous improvement, sense of urgency, team development, organization/planning, expectations/ accountability, and resolving problems. Questions are asked on the grass-roots survey of all associates to address each of these competencies and to determine the manager's capability and areas of weakness. Here are the questions from the actual grass-roots survey related to each key leadership competency:

Communication:
  1. My manager keeps me informed?
  2. My manager communicates in a clear and concise manner?

Developing Others
  3. My manager empowers me to make decisions and take risks?
  4. My manager teaches me and shares his/her knowledge?

Motivation
  5. My manager recognizes the accomplishments of associates?
  6. My manager challenges people to reach their full potential?

Customer Focused
  7. My manager seeks better ways to serve the customers?
  8. My manager practices the "10-foot rule" with customers and associates?

Listening
  9. My manager asks questions if messages are unclear or confusing?

10. My manager actively listens to me and others?

Continuous Improvement

11. My manager supports and encourages challenging the status quo?
12. My manager fosters/supports new ideas to improve the company?

Sense of Urgency

13. My manager responds in a timely manner to challenges placed before him/her?
14. My manager follows the sundown rule (same-day response)?

Team Development

15. My manager encourages cooperation between work groups?
16. My manager serves as a fully participating member?

Organization/Planning

17. My manager sets appropriate priorities based upon current demands?
18. My manager develops a plan to accomplish objectives?

Expectations/Accountability

19. My manager assumes responsibility for his or her work?
20. My manager measures results against pre-agreed standards and expectations?

Resolving Problems

21. My manager believes in fact finding?
22. My manager uses quality processes to resolve short- and long-term problems?
23. My manager believes in and supports the open-door policy for all associates?

Comments are also requested from associates and are compiled into a list under the heading *opportunities* for negative comments and a list of supportive feedback under the heading *positive comments*. Each of the questions is scored on a 0 to 3 scale with 3 being *exceeds my expectations*, 2 being *meets my expectations*, 1 being *does not meet my expectations*, and 0 being *did not answer the question*. The results are compiled by question numerically based on the input of all participating associates, and an overall score is tabulated. Because the survey is done anonymously, the feedback can be very direct and associates are free to say exactly what they think.

Here's how one store manager describes how a grass-roots survey is conducted:

> The district manager comes into the store and the store manager goes to lunch or he or she takes an afternoon off. They pass out a pretty generic survey to the associates, who evaluate the store manager on various points. The associates can also write comments which are completely anonymous. The survey is compiled and presented to the store manager at his or her annual performance evaluation. If there are any issues, then a meeting is held with the associates to follow up and discuss them.

Discussion areas may include: the manager, pay, benefits, scheduling, treatment, career opportunities, training, communication, diversity, safety, customer service, teamwork, integrity and ethics, and policies and procedures. The goal with grass-roots surveys is to identify concerns at a local level. In the group meetings a local manager reviews the results of the survey with all of the associates and asks them to discuss their feelings about specific problem areas identified in order to come up with solutions. In some cases the manager provides information to help associates better understand why something of concern is done the way it is done. Not all issues are solved to the satisfaction of everyone in attendance, but everyone walks out of these meetings knowing they have been given the chance to say what is on their minds.

The *open-door policy* at Wal-Mart provides the associates with an internal mechanism for expressing their concerns when they feel they have been unfairly treated. Feelings of unfair treatment may be a result of a concern or question on issues such as associate relations, harassment, discrimination, integrity/ethics, safety, waste, or policy. The policy encourages associates to bring their concerns to management in order to resolve important issues as they arise. There are several steps to the open-door process that lead all the way up the management chain of command to the company's president.

At step 1, Wal-Mart's associates are encouraged to discuss their open-door issues or concerns privately with their immediate supervisor. Because most problems involve the immediate work group, the majority of problems can be resolved at this level. The associate has the opportunity to sit down with his or her immediate supervisor to review the situation first. If the immediate supervisor is the issue or is personally involved in the issue, associates are encouraged to proceed immediately to step 2. An investigation ensues at each level of the open-door policy, and an answer is returned to the associate, in many cases immediately or within a reasonable period of time.

If the associate is not satisfied with his or her immediate supervisor's response, at step 1, he or she may appeal that decision by proceeding to discuss their concern with the next level of management. Again the issue is investigated, and an answer is returned as quickly as possible. The open-door steps at Wal-Mart could involve meeting with the store manager, district manager, regional vice-president of operations, and even the president/CEO.

Sam Walton expected associates to utilize the open-door policy, and he was concerned if a store *didn't* have recent examples of associate's using it. More often than not, Mr. Sam would encourage his managers to err on the side of the associate, who came forward by solving the complaint in favor of the associate, in essence "letting them win." Mr. Sam's goal was fair treatment and to show he meant it, he would bend over backward to support the associate's position if it was reasonable. An associate who had a successful experience using the open-door policy would go back to his or her work group and tell everyone about the success. Sam Walton's goal was to give the associates a viable internal problem resolution vehicle.

Daily meetings are conducted each day for each shift in the 24-hour stores to keep the associates informed about what the priorities are for that day or week. Mr. Sam used to conduct his daily meetings in the front of the store by the cash registers in full view of his customers. Today, some managers continue his tradition, whereas others hold meetings in the break room or merchandise warehouse off the sales floor. Current company news is reviewed and items of local interest are discussed so all associates have the most current information impacting their work lives. These meetings are brief stand-up meetings that allow enough time for associates to express their own questions or concerns. As Sam Walton would do, local managers always lead the associates in an enthusiastic Wal-Mart cheer at every meeting.

Safety is a major concern in a work environment with so many employees, so much merchandise, and so many customers milling about. The challenges are endless. There are safety issues in the parking lot, in the backroom warehouse, and on the sales floor, and for this reason safety training is an ongoing and endless effort. Merchandising shelves can be dangerous, spills of liquids can cause slips and falls, and even collecting shopping carts from the parking lot can be dangerous. There is no better way for managers to show concern for the associates than to show sincere concern for their personal safety.

Exit interviews are used by Wal-Mart's managers to capture the reasons why associates are leaving the company so local managers can develop strategies to improve retention. Sam Walton valued long-term associates and he wanted to do what he could to counteract turnover. Consistently exit-interviewing all departing associates is how Wal-Mart's managers clarify the trends in their turnover to help them design turnover reduction strategies and tactics. By asking people specific questions and gathering feedback at a time when they have nothing to lose, you will learn the true reasons behind why people are leaving. Typically, it isn't for any singular reason; people quit jobs for all kinds of reasons. They also stay with companies for very specific reasons.

The goal of exit interviewing at Wal-Mart is to learn from the past so that local managers don't repeat the same mistakes over and over again in the future. Identifying and understanding the reasons why people are leaving allow managers to develop a proactive retention strategy to avoid further attrition.

Attendance and punctuality are essential to achieving optimal productivity and customer service at Wal-Mart. When associates don't show up for scheduled work, the entire team suffers the consequences. Individual attendance issues are dealt with through performance coaching. Systemic issues with attendance and tardiness across an entire work group indicate a bigger problem with morale and leadership. Associates who are happy and enjoy their work have a tendency to show up for work each and every day. Poor attendance impacts customer service, merchandising, and team morale. By monitoring attendance, Mr. Sam figured out another way to identify morale problems in a store or distribution center. Once identified, an action plan had to be developed by finding out the reasons why associates weren't coming to work. When numbers of associates are missing work, Mr. Sam knew it wasn't an indication of bad associates but more an indication of a breakdown in leadership.

Retention and turnover strategy development starts by gaining an understanding of the reasons behind why associates are leaving in the first place, while simultaneously figuring out why long-term local associates have decided to remain employed. Just like at Wal-Mart, I think many of us would agree that there are cases where some turnover is actually advantageous. Did you ever experience relief when one of your employees quit? So there are cases where voluntary or targeted turnover can actually be a good thing. There is a point at which too much turnover becomes a business disruption at Wal-Mart, and it is at that point when not having someone in place today disrupts the continuity of service to its customers.

Mr. Sam understood that turnover of trained associates negatively impacted everything he was trying to accomplish at Wal-Mart. He knew how much easier every manager's job would be if he or she could retain a team of well-trained, highly productive, and qualified people. I can almost hear him saying to his management team, "If you can keep your turnover low, life would be so good you could hardly stand it!" In a high-turnover environment, managers are thrown into a vicious cycle of hiring and turnover, leaving managers with very little time to address concerns about training, safety, customer service, or associate relations. Every location has an equilibrium they have to reach in which retention and turnover are balanced to allow the day-to-day operation of the business. Mr. Sam knew that when turnover is high, morale suffers and when morale is down, customer service suffers. The answer to improving retention for local managers may be to go back to the basics of servant leadership by listening and responding to the concerns of associates.

Performance coaching is a key element of Wal-Mart's overall performance management strategy. Mr. Sam taught his leadership team to coach those who are not performing, aggressively because there are some people who work in every organization who try to figure out the lowest acceptable performance level. Unacceptable performance in their minds means the point beyond which company managers begin to formally counsel employees, which after several defined steps (verbal, written, final, and termination), can lead to termination. Mr. Sam wasn't shy about taking on nonperforming associates and if need be moving them right out the door. One of the reasons he did it was for morale purposes. If you want to give your good and great performers in any organization a reason to continue to perform, they have to see leaders dealing with those who aren't performing. Mr. Sam taught company leaders to deal with people in an evenhanded manner. He recognized those who performed their jobs well, thus, accentuating the positive, while at the same time he eliminated the negative by dealing quickly and directly with those who weren't performing satisfactorily. The secret of performance coaching I learned from Sam Walton is that you have to give your good performers a reason to continue doing a good job by showing them you are addressing the performance issues of the nonperformers.

SMART evaluations are used to review the performance of the managers and associates at Wal-Mart. In a store or distribution center the goals of the top manager are cascaded down to everyone else to ensure all are focused on achieving the most important overall goals of that facility. SMART is actually a goal-setting acronym that stands for *s*pecific, *m*easurable, *a*ction-oriented, *r*ealistic. and *t*ime-bound. *Specific* refers to the performance or a behavior that is specifically related to an associate's job. *Measurable* indicates the associate's performance is above or below a goal that is easy to measure using a variety of accessible sources such as budget, quality, and quantity. *Action-oriented* refers to the fact that the associate must be able to do something personally to move toward the goal. This means the goal must be something the associate is directly responsible for and can only be accomplished through his or her efforts. *Realistic* is a way of setting people up to succeed. Consideration is given as to whether the associate can be expected to accomplish a goal given all of his or her other responsibilities and limited resources. *Time-bound* simply means can the goal be accomplished within the performance review period. SMART goal setting is designed to focus associates on accomplishment each and every day.

By setting goals and holding managers and associates accountable to them, high performance levels are achieved. There are three phases to Sam Walton's old-style MBO (management by objectives) review process: goal setting, progress reviews, and a year-end performance review. The goal setting or performance planning is done at the beginning of the year as a collaborative effort. Managers and associates establish site, department, and individual goals for the upcoming year. Goals are established around measurable criteria like quality, quantity, cost, timeliness, use of resources, and customer satisfaction. Progress reviews occur throughout the year and serve to measure and document progress toward achievement of annual goals. Input is received and included in the review from internal as well as external customers.

The year-end evaluation or performance review serves as a final assessment of performance against goals and includes an open discussion of competencies, strengths, and development needs as provided by solicited feedback from customers. Particular attention is paid to associate relations in appraising management performance by reviewing associates' input on the performance of their own supervisors.

It is clear that Sam Walton valued people, and the various communication tactics I've just reviewed are a good indication of his sincerity. However, imagine for just a moment the kinds of questions Sam Walton might ask a store leadership team or distribution center leadership team on one of his store visits. The following is a list of questions I think Sam Walton would ask to determine whether or not his managers were listening, responding, and showing the associates they care:

- Is there evidence that associates are comfortable using the open-door policy?
- Are the associates supportive of every member of the management team?
- Do any managers' names keep coming up again and again, indicating a problem, during open-door discussions or grass-root meetings with associates?
- Are open-door issues and recommendations followed through on by management quickly and thoroughly and then communicated to associates?
- Are daily meetings held with all associates on every work shift?
- When associates bring up concerns, does a member of management respond to those concerns immediately or follow up with a prompt answer?

- Have the issues that were brought up by associates during the grass-roots survey and annual meeting been addressed and corrected?
- Do associates believe company policies are consistently and fairly enforced without favoritism?
- Have associates questioned the reasons for receiving performance coaching or challenged a termination?
- Are jobs posted so that everyone has an opportunity to be considered?
- Do the most qualified associates receive promotional opportunities?
- Does the leadership team reflect a diverse cross section of people?
- Does the salaried management staff reflect associates who were promoted from hourly paid positions?
- Is adequate training being conducted so that associates are able to perform their jobs?
- Does the management team focus on safety as a priority?
- What is the accident and injury history and what are we doing about it?
- What is the current absenteeism rate and why?
- What is the turnover rate of associates and is it too high?
- What is the retention rate of the associates who have stayed with the company and why?
- Are exit interviews being conducted and, if so, what kinds of trends are indicated?
- How do the associates' wages compare to comparable jobs at other retailers in the area?
- Are the performance goals of managers and associates being met?

Think about Sam Walton visiting a store and asking the management team these kinds of tough associate relations questions. It shows you how serious he really was about listening to people and being responsive to their needs. Like a "human inventory," you too can use this same list of questions for your organization to determine whether of not your management team is really listening and responding to employees, coaching their performance, and showing they care.

I asked one of Wal-Mart's former store managers to share a final lesson he had learned from Sam Walton about how to treat people, and here is what he said:

> I was taught a great lesson, when I first went to work for Wal-Mart, about dealing with associates. I was told to imagine Sam Walton is looking over my shoulder as I talked to an associate, and if he was, how would I talk to or treat that associate? Under those circumstances you wouldn't be rude, mad, or angry. I've taught that same lesson to the managers who reported to me. I asked them to imagine how they'd communicate with an employee if Mr. Sam, the man who signed their paycheck, was looking over their shoulder.

EXCEED EXPECTATIONS
of Customers and Others

The difference between achieving good
versus outstanding results in life
all comes down to your level
of commitment to excellence.

S am Walton flipped Wal-Mart's organizational pyramid, making the most important employees at Wal-Mart those in the stores providing service directly to the customers. But interestingly enough, it wasn't just the store associates who were expected to provide great service to the company's customers. Everyone in the organization was focused on customer service, whether they worked in the headquarters, distribution, fleet, or stores because at Wal-Mart everybody, in every department, is expected to act like a retail merchant. Mr. Sam referred to his employees as "associates," his managers as "coaches," and his customers as "friends or neighbors." The reason the term "associate" is used rather than the term "employee" is to reinforce the fact that Mr. Sam's employees were business partners and business owners, in other words, his "business associates." Sam Walton believed in treating his customers like neighbors or guests and his loyal associates like family. If you think these terms are simply a clever use of language, think again. These changes in terminology are significant at Wal-Mart, and their use changes the way its people interact. There really is an expectation of a higher level of relationship and interaction between its managers and its associates and in turn between its associates and its customers. This shift in the way people are treated has created extraordinary loyalty among Mr. Sam's team of associates, which made all the difference in how consumers were treated when they entered his stores.

Sam Walton's eighth success secret for achieving remarkable results is *"EXCEED EXPECTATIONS of customers and others."* Mr. Sam established his "Wal-Mart way" of exceeding the expectations of his customers long before the management consulting service gurus latched onto it as a new wave idea for business success. In the early days he didn't refer to his service standard as exceeding the customers' expectations because exceeding was already his standard for the normal day-to-day service he expected his associates to provide to his customers, always! In other words, Mr. Sam didn't know any other way of serving customers other than trying to exceed their expectations.

He understood that if he treated customers well, gave them what they wanted, and even a little more, they were likely to return again and again to shop in his stores. To illustrate this point, here's a great story a store manager shared with me about the lengths Mr. Sam taught him to go to in satisfying customers:

> I had a customer who brought a coffeemaker in to exchange it or to get a refund. We couldn't find it in our item file. I happened to notice that item in the K-Mart ad that same week because we kept all the competitor's ads at the service desk. I told the woman who was returning the coffeemaker that hers was a K-Mart special model manufactured uniquely for K-Mart. She said she was sorry she didn't realize that and she said she would take it back to them. I said don't take it back over there; we're going to give you this amount in the ad back for it, because the next time you buy a coffeemaker I want you to buy it here and not across the street.

This story illustrates the extraordinary lengths Mr. Sam expected company leaders to go to satisfy customers.

Mr. Sam taught all of the associates to let the customers know how much everyone at Wal-Mart appreciated their business by welcoming them into the store and thanking them as they left. When associates made a mistake in their dealings with a customer, they were expected to accept responsibility for their mistake and offer an apology. When customers experienced problems with products, he taught service desk associates to provide a merchandise exchange or money back with no questions asked. Mr. Sam believed that his standard of "satisfaction guaranteed" made all the difference in the world in Wal-Mart's relationship with its customers. Far more than words on a sign, "satisfaction guaranteed" at Wal-Mart is an indisputable customer service contract with the consumer. One of Sam Walton's store managers shared this product guarantee story with me:

> One of the lessons Mr. Sam taught me was "taking care of the customer." He said that if the customer buys a lawnmower and they use it for three years and they drag it back into the store with the wheels falling off and otherwise falling apart and they ask to return it, don't question them about why they returned it! He said just take care of the customer. Because that customer never would have brought it back to you if they felt they had gotten their money's worth out of it. He said just take care of that customer because that customer is going to come back and spend more money with you. If you make them mad and you don't take care of them, they are going to go somewhere else to spend their money the next time and the next time and the next time. Always remember to take care of the customer because 97 percent of your customers are good, honest hardworking people and maybe 3 percent are dishonest. Why penalize 97 percent of your customers if only 3 percent are going to do you wrong?"

Mr. Sam's goal was for Wal-Mart to be known for its legendary customer service.

Providing great customer service continues to provide Wal-Mart with a tremendous competitive advantage in the marketplace to this day. Like so many things in Mr. Sam's unique business strategy, customer service at Wal-Mart is one of his tactics designed to separate the company from the rest of the retail pack. Great service, coupled with great products, selection, and prices, lures his customers back again and again to shop in his stores. Sam Walton built his business by attracting customers with a combination of great customer service and always having the lowest prices. His goal was to have everything the consumer could possibly want under one roof, what he called "one-stop shopping," so there was no reason for his customers to shop anywhere else.

One of the biggest challenges an organization faces as it grows is in simply communicating its own service standards to its own people. Wal-Mart meets this daunting task through an ongoing barrage of messages, which include the use of folklore, stories, slogans, and Wal-Mart truisms. Here is one example of how Mr. Sam communicated Wal-Mart's customer service commandments to his associates:

> Customers are...
> - The most important people in our business.
> - Not dependent on us; we are completely dependent on them.
> - Doing us a favor when they shop at our stores; we are not doing them a favor by providing customer service.
> - An important part of our business; they are insiders not outsiders.
> - Not people with whom we argue, match wits, or get angry.
> - People who bring us their wants, and it is our job to meet their needs.
> - Not cold statistics; they are people with emotions and feelings just like us.
> - Deserving of the most courteous and attentive service we can provide.
> - The people who buy our products and pay our salaries.
> - The lifeblood of our company and every other business out there.

By clearly communicating his expectations to his own people Sam Walton prepared them to provide the highest level of service to his customers.

Mr. Sam believed that the customer was "the boss" and was even quoted as having said, "There is only one boss. The customer. And he or she can fire everybody in the company from the chairman on down, simply by spending his or her money some-where else." To satisfy the needs of "the boss," Mr. Sam dedicated himself to trying new ideas and new approaches to customer ser-vice, product promotion, product purchasing, expenses, and pric-ing, which ultimately led him on a journey into total quality.

Many small business owners don't use total quality methods, and many don't understand the value of total quality principles. As much as anything Sam Walton's knowledge and use of total quality and his ability to teach others around him those principles have created a lopsided competitive advantage. Mr. Sam's per-sonal commitment to innovation, continuous improvement, and continuous learning started years before the total quality move-ment even existed. When professional total quality principles were first introduced to Sam Walton, on a trip he made to Japan, he realized he had already been applying many of those principles himself for years. Mr. Sam already believed in constantly tweak-ing the current way of doing things in search of breakthrough ideas to improve operational efficiency, lower costs, and improve customer service. It was for that reason that the Japanese contin-uous improvement concept *kaizen*, seemed to make the biggest impression on him. *Kaizen* translated means, "to take something apart and put it back together again in a better way." He came back from that trip energized in the belief that he needed to teach the managers and associates at Wal-Mart the professional princi-ples of total quality that he had personally learned the hard way, over the years, through painstaking trial and error. The secret behind continuously improving Wal-Mart's operation is the tire-less pursuit of small improvements in processes that over time will lead to big improvements. Chairman Sam became the "king of kaizen" in his never-ending quest to continuously improve every area of the Wal-Mart kingdom.

He welcomed total quality partnerships with Malcolm Baldrige award-winning companies like Procter and Gamble (P&G). The Malcolm Baldrige Award Program is designed to encourage American companies and workers to continuously improve their operations. Sam Walton had visions of Wal-Mart becoming the first retailer to win the prestigious Malcolm Baldrige Quality Award. It was those partnerships with excellent companies like P&G that allowed Mr. Sam to crystallize his beliefs about continuous improvement. The systematic professional quality training programs offered by P&G allowed him for the first time to standardize the teaching of quality improvement processes across all of Wal-Mart. The principles taught, as it turns out, were principles he had already been practicing and that he had personally believed in for years.

Sam Walton was so committed to quality at Wal-Mart that he developed pillars of total quality that were taught at the company's Walton Institute at the University of Arkansas. His pillars included empowerment, diversity, expense control, customer service, technology, productivity, and continuous improvement. When Mr. Sam's official total quality movement finally standardized training of the company's managers and associates, Wal-Mart raised its game to a whole new level. The synergy created by so many people working together as a team toward the common goal to improve everything is an advantage that is hard for competitors to beat. Company leaders and associates remain committed to finding small ways to improve the company every day that ultimately lead to big improvements over time. Commitment to continuous improvement, and the resulting team synergy, has made a major ongoing impact on the success of an already successful company.

The next ongoing and daunting task Mr. Sam faced was in determining what to sell in his stores. As part of his barrage of messages he taught everyone the importance of talking with the customers. The secret to his one-stop shopping success was in simply asking the consumers what they wanted and then giving them exactly what they had told him they desired. He determined his customers wanted a great assortment of quality merchandise, everyday low prices, product guarantees, terrific service, friendly employees, a convenient location with store hours to match their busy schedules, a large free parking lot, and enough cashiers to get them out of the store when they were finished shopping. By identifying everything that was important to his customers, he designed his stores to create a positive shopping experience with the goal of meeting or exceeding the needs of his customers. Mr. Sam never lost sight of the importance of customer input and it remains one of the company's most important values.

Wal-Mart's customer service in its stores is legendary, and that is no accident. Sam Walton established three basic beliefs upon which he built his business:

1. Respect for each and every individual.
2. Providing excellent service to the customer.
3. Striving for excellence in every aspect of the business.

He developed his three core beliefs back in 1962, and those beliefs remain cultural touchstones for the executives, managers, and associates of the company to this day. Check out company web sites and you'll find his three basic beliefs are still practiced around the world.

When Sam Walton said he wanted to provide excellent service, he meant it. I remember hearing him say, "Let's be friendly to our customers by offering them a smile and a shopping cart when they enter our stores. Let's give service above and beyond what our customers expect. Let's exceed our customers' expectations. If we do that, they'll come back again and again." Sam Walton understood the value of providing great service to the enhancement of the shopping experience for his customers. He used to tell the associates, "I want you to promise that whenever you come within 10 feet of a customer, you will look 'em in the eye, greet 'em, and ask 'em if you can help 'em." This edict from Sam Walton became a customer service standard called the *10-foot rule*, which remains one of the most important service requirements of company associates to this day.

Mr. Sam wanted everyone in his stores to keep a steady focus on the number 1 priority, which is exceeding the customers' expectations. Clearly, he believed that each sales transaction was important, but even more important was the idea of nurturing and creating a customer for life. That's why he believed in treating customers like VIPs when they entered his stores. He used the same standards of treatment for his customers that any of us would use in the way we treat our best friends or beloved family members. Mr. Sam was obsessed with customer service, and he expected everyone else in the company to embrace and share that same obsession. He went to great lengths to satisfy customers, as this story from one of his former store managers illustrates:

> One of the things that Mr. Sam did that really had a big impact on the business was the service desk. He said it doesn't matter whether you have a receipt or not, it doesn't matter when you bought it, it doesn't matter whether anything is wrong with it or not, if you don't like it and you don't want it anymore, you bring it back and we will give you your money back with a smile. Mr. Sam put the service desk at the very front of the store where every customer coming in the door could watch the disgruntled customers who were bringing things back getting

taken care of. Everybody else (in retail) had their service desk or return center stuck away in some back corner where no one could see them and no one could see those customers being dealt with.

[Here's an example of how Wal-Mart handled customer merchandise returns.] An old gentleman came into my store to return a pair of worn-out kid's tennis shoes that were dirty and tattered. He said his grandson couldn't wear the shoes because they didn't fit him. The service desk called me up to explain to me he wanted to exchange them for another larger pair. The service desk associate told me the shoes were worn out and his grandson has outgrown them and now he wants a new pair. I went over and talked to the gentleman, who said his grandson had worn the shoes for a little while and he can't wear them anymore and he couldn't afford to buy shoes every time you turn around. I just want to get a pair of shoes that will fit him. I believed he wasn't trying to take me for a ride; he was just trying to get his grandson a pair of shoes that would fit. So I exchanged those old beat-up shoes for a new pair of shoes; I knew that's what Sam Walton would have done. Now did he take us for a ride? Did he get something he wasn't necessarily entitled to? Probably. Do we have a customer who left the store that day who is tickled to death with Wal-Mart, who will probably come back there again to shop rather than go somewhere else? Absolutely!

This story illustrates the level of Mr. Sam's commitment to customer service. If Sam Walton had heard this story, he would have applauded this manager's commitment to providing outstanding service to that customer. In all likelihood, he would have told this story to all of the company's leaders at a Saturday morning meeting to reinforce his commitment to the philosophy that customer satisfaction is guaranteed.

To accomplish his goal of exceeding expectations, Sam Walton required that everyone at his company focus on improving service to the customers in the stores; it didn't matter what department you worked in or what you did for the company. After his Saturday morning meetings, Mr. Sam would hold a separate new product review meeting at which several of the company's merchandise buyers would present one new product idea to him and a cross section of leaders from across all home office functions. You could tell that Sam Walton really enjoyed picking products for the stores and that he wanted everyone else to share his enthusiasm. Mr. Sam, in full merchant mode, would question each buyer about the cost, price point, and margin of the product he or she presented while the rest of us watched. He would then ask everyone in attendance what we thought of each product immediately after it had been presented by the buyer. He was asking us if we thought it should be added to the merchandise assortment going into the stores.

I can vividly remember Mr. Sam parading across the stage with a product hoisted above his head asking everyone, "What do you think?" If the majority cheered, indicating the consensus of opinion was positive, that particular product would be added to the merchandise assortment. If the majority jeered, Mr. Sam would tell that buyer to go find another better product. This bit of Wal-Mart Theater was orchestrated by Mr. Sam to teach everyone the importance of selecting the right products for the stores. With respect to product purchasing, he used to say, "You eat what you kill," which means if you *bought it,* you *own it* and you've got to *sell it.* He wanted everyone to take ownership of the products going into the stores, especially his buyers, and by so doing he taught everyone to think like a merchant.

Sam Walton believed the combination of great service and everyday low prices would attract customers just like bees to honey. He was right. Along the way he tried to exceed his customer's expectations with an ever-changing mix of products and too-good-to-be-true bargains, all merchandised in humongous quantities to ensure they were never out of stock. Customers wander the store as if in a discount-induced shopping trance, loading their carts to the brim with impulsively purchased items they just can't live without! The products, selection, merchandising, and low prices are so attractive to customers that they simply stop shopping anywhere else. The result for competitors can be devastating as their previously loyal customers switch their loyalties to shop for Wal-Mart's every-day low-priced products.

Because so many of Wal-Mart's competitors carry similar products, Mr. Sam wanted to distinguish Wal-Mart by not only offering the lowest possible prices but also by having the best service of any retailer. Over the years, consumer expectations of service have risen; they have become less tolerant of poor service; and they will stop doing business with organizations offering lousy service. Mr. Sam's goal was to *always* have the best prices and to *always* have the best service.

One of Mr. Sam's store managers shared with me the importance of the term *always* to the Wal-Mart service culture:

> The use of *always* has taken on a life of its own at Wal-Mart over the years. Originally, it came into use during the late 1980s. As you are aware, Wal-Mart came on the scene in small towns practicing a new kind of retail. Rather than the then-standard practice of pricing everything at the manufacturer's suggested retail price (MSRP) and then running event sales to draw traffic and volume, Mr. Sam adopted the everyday

low price (EDLP) philosophy. He did not try to compete with advertising and gimmicks. He kept that money on the bottom line. Since he was not spending money on expensive newspaper and radio ads, he could afford to take a lower margin on his merchandise—and EDLP was born. No need to wait for a sale because Wal-Mart's items were on sale *every day* and, compared to the prices of every other retailer, they were!

While Wal-Mart was opening stores slowly and with a low profile, this strategy worked. A store would open; people would come and see what it was all about and fall in love with this new pricing philosophy. However, as we began opening stores more quickly and more prominently, we found that the term *everyday low prices* just did not resonate with the public at large, in terms of building an image. So, in (I think) 1988, Wal-Mart adopted the use of *always* and implemented its first major advertising campaign. In-store signage was converted in every store overnight to coincide with the launch of the ad campaign. Now, instead of proclaiming *everyday low prices*, the message was "We will have the lowest price—not just during some sales—but *always!*" No need for customers to search through the weekly ads and plan their shopping trips by going from store to store to get the best bargains; now there was Wal-Mart, and you could count on Wal-Mart to have the low price *always*. It just was a better "connect" for the average person.

It was such a success that it has simply become ingrained in the company. *always* has become the mantra—for customer service, in stock, store standards—you name it. It has even become the tag line for the Wal-Mart cheer.

Mr. Sam used a variety of advertising slogans over the years but none has been quite as effective as *Always Low Prices*.

In addition to his strategies for "always low prices" and "always great service," Mr. Sam had another unique strategy he used for always selecting the right products for his stores. Using an outside-in approach to product selection, he had Wal-Mart's buyers travel out to the stores and spend time talking with company managers, associates, and customers in search of customer-driven product ideas. Buyers also spent time shopping competitor's stores in search of the next blockbuster new product. By traveling constantly, Wal-Mart's buyers clearly have their finger on the pulse of their customers. They understand the product desires of the customers and they are willing to take risks by buying aggressively to satisfy those needs. A smart buyer who traveled out to the stores would return to Bentonville with all kinds of great product ideas to share with other members of the home office buying team.

Mr. Sam also used an outside-in approach to determine how his customers perceived his stores in general and the level of customer service in particular. To accomplish this monumental task, customers at every store are periodically surveyed to determine their opinions on 10 key questions about their local store. Here are the 10 areas covered in the customer survey:

- Likelihood of revisiting the store in the next four weeks.
- Are the employees helpful and knowledgeable?
- Is there a wide selection of products?
- Do you feel Wal-Mart has low prices?
- Are you able to return items easily?
- Do you find the employees to be friendly?
- Is the store clean?
- Are the products you need in stock?
- Ability to check-out quickly.
- Number of visits to that store in the past 4 weeks.

These customer surveys are taken very seriously and the results from each individual store are compared to company standards.

Mr. Sam considered customers the lifeblood of the company and for this reason his customer service survey provided a quick means for intervention if the local level of service was slipping.

One of the problems Mr. Sam identified with teaching merchant skills to the people who worked in his retail stores was that these skills were actually negatively impacted by centralized buying. Add to that the fact that as merchandise is flowing into the stores, every square foot of shelf space is managed with computer software, ensuring a place to display existing and new products. Centralization of buying and managing shelf space with computer software is a necessity when you have so many stores and so many products. Unfortunately, managers and associates had for the most part lost the responsibility for picking products on a local level as they were forced to implement product strategies developed by merchandise buyers in Bentonville. The problem this created from Mr. Sam's point of view is that his managers and associates in the stores needed to learn the cause-and-effect relationship of selecting a great product, displaying it well, and watching it "blow" off the shelves. This is one of the most important skills of all mom-and-pop merchants who control purchasing, displaying, and selling merchandise. Mr. Sam considered these merchant skills vitally important to anyone working in retail. To address this issue, Sam Walton created a program called *volume producing item* (VPI), designed to teach basic merchant skills to his managers and associates alike. A manager who worked with Sam Walton described the program:

> It's a requirement for department managers and assistant managers to turn in a VPI (volume producing item) product recommendation at the beginning of every month. It's also available to any associate in the store who wants to pick an item and promote it. So every month you've got people build-

ing creative merchandise displays and creatively trying to find ways to promote their item. One VPI success story that comes to mind is about a young part-time associate, who was in high school at the time, who worked there nights and weekends in the pet department. He took bird cages that we typically sold in the box up on the very top shelf, and for that reason you didn't move a lot of them. He took the time to put a couple of dozen of them together himself and built a big end cap (end-of-aisle merchandise display) display out of them. He got some stuffed animal birds from the toy department to put in the cages and then got a tape recorder and a tape of bird sounds to play to draw attention to the bird cages. He ended up selling the heck out of those bird cages. That kind of creativity and that kind of ownership came from a guy who worked part time and who goes to high school. That's what the VPI program is all about.

At the end of the month he won the VPI award for my store. The first place winner got a congratulatory certificate, a $25.00 gift certificate and a great job pin. If you won four great job pins you could turn them in for a share of Wal-Mart stock. The second-place winner would get a congratulatory certificate and a $15.00 gift certificate. Finally, the third-place winner would get a congratulatory certificate and a $10.00 gift certificate. First-place winners at the store got submitted to the district level, and the district manager would choose one winner for that district. If you won the district, you won another great job pin and a $50.00 gift certificate and the winner got to go to lunch with the district manager; you'd also get submitted to the regional level. If you won at the regional level, you got a $100.00 gift certificate and another great job pin. Each year an annual VPI winner was selected for the single best VPI product, and the winner of that award got a vacation trip to a place like Alaska, with his or her family. On a monthly basis, all of the regional VPI winner's product ideas, from every district across the region, were published in a brochure and sent out to all the stores. The goal of the VPI program was to teach merchant skills.

The company has the same focus on merchant skills and customer service in all of its stores all over the planet. Visit any of Walt-Mart's Web sites in Germany, Korea, the United Kingdom, China, Brazil, Argentina, Mexico, Puerto Rico, Japan, and Canada, and you'll find evidence of Mr. Sam's original merchant and service standards. By reading Sam Walton's standards on Wal-Mart's Web sites, associates, prospective employees, and customers learn the difference in how Wal-Mart approaches its relationship with customers compared with everyone else. Here is how the Wal-Mart Web site describes Sam Walton's original merchant and service standards for his associates in countries around the world:

> "Service to Our Customers" is the single most important job we have. Our customer service at Wal-Mart, distinguishes us from the rest of our competitors. If we provide outstanding service, with a goal of exceeding our customers' expectations, we will be handsomely rewarded. Talk to our customers and ask them what they want, to help us determine the right products to sell in our stores. Don't take your customers for granted; treat them with respect and sincere appreciation. If you make a mistake own up to it; don't make excuses, just apologize, accept responsibility and move on. Always remember, and stand behind, the two most important words of Wal-Mart's customer service standard for which we must always be known: "satisfaction guaranteed."

> "The Customer is the Real Boss," at Wal-Mart. Every one of us who works in a retail store is in actuality employed by its customers. If you do a good job of meeting their needs they'll buy our merchandise and we'll stay in business. If we don't meet their needs, they will simply go elsewhere, in essence "fir-

ing us" in favor of spending their money somewhere else. The customer is "the boss," and customer service success is measured by whether or not our customers decide to shop in our stores again and again. Provide "aggressive service" and make certain every single customer is satisfied every time.

"Satisfaction Guaranteed" is one of the first and most important service standards initiated at Wal-Mart and it sets the tone for all of the rest of our service related philosophies. If a customer has a problem with merchandise purchased in our stores let's take care of that problem promptly. Treat them the way that you would want to be treated and be just as pleasant accepting a return as we were when the customer bought the item originally. Ask the customer, "What would you like us to do and then just do it!" Give them a choice of a merchandise exchange or a full refund. In some cases we will even offer to repair the item. Let's do everything we can to satisfy our customers. The way we handle customers with a problem creates one of the best opportunities we have to meet and even exceed their expectations. If we do it right we'll build customer loyalty and they'll come back to shop in our stores again and again.

"The Sundown Rule" is another way of saying don't put off until tomorrow what you *should* do today. This means getting back to people who leave messages the day those messages are received. If a customer calls, get back to them today. If a fellow associate contacts you, show them the respect they deserve by getting back to them before the day is over. If one of our suppliers contacts you, treat them like a business partner by following up with them immediately. When you respond to the needs of people quickly it shows how much you care. This standard of service sets our service a bar higher than most and by doing so demonstrates our commitment to providing better service than anyone else.

"Aggressive Hospitality" is the Wal-Mart way of meeting and exceeding the needs of our customers. If one of our customers asks you for help in finding a product take them right to that department and show them where that merchandise is located. Make our customers feel welcome by looking them in the eye, smiling at them, and enthusiastically greeting them. Approach every customer with whom you come in contact. We call this standard the "10 foot rule." Be sure to use the names of the customers you know.

"The People Greeter" is a great example of our aggressive approach to service. I got the idea from one of our stores down in Louisiana. Their version of aggressive hospitality is called "lagniappe" which is defined as giving the customer a little something extra that they don't expect but that we at Wal-Mart know they are going to like. Lagniappe can be a smile, a greeting, saying thank-you, providing a shopping cart or helping the customer find a product they are looking for. The people greeter's warm welcome is the first impression our customers have of our stores so let's make it a good one.

Obviously, Sam Walton was passionate about providing superior customer service. Regardless of his customers' expectations, he always tried to think of ways to meet and exceed those customer expectations. His goal was to create a shopping experience that was so positive and convenient and so far superior to that offered by other retailers that the customer wouldn't want to shop anywhere else. Mr. Sam wanted the shopping experience at Wal-Mart to be memorable for his customers; thus, the company introduced a concept called *retailtainment*. Retailtainment is the combination of the word "retail" and the word "entertainment." In business terms it is combining Wal-Mart's retailing business with entertainment. Retailtainment increases customer loyalty and sales by creating a fun shopping experience for customers. Retailtainment, from a customer perspective, makes the shopping experience more interesting. The idea is to differentiate Wal-Mart's shopping experience from that of its competitors.

Unlike product samplings or product demonstrations, retailtainment events drive customers to visit specific areas of the store to participate in contests, games, and free product giveaways. The Wal-Mart Korea Web site describes three recent retailtainment events as "guess the weight of a banana," "throwing ring competition," and "cartoon character drawing contest." The winners receive small and inexpensive gifts such as flowers and chocolate. The events are fun for everyone involved and drive impulse purchasing of the featured item. The goal of retailtainment is to sell products while at the same time creating an entertaining shopping experience for the consumer. Here's an insight on retailtainment provided by a Wal-Mart store manager:

> When we launched the Harry Potter videos, we had an associate in the stores dressed up like Harry Potter at a table so the kids could come up to him and get a free sticker; some glasses that looked like Harry Potter's, a magic wand and a coloring book. We did the same thing with Bob the Builder in the toy department. In sporting goods we did line winding clinics, or we'd have a professional bass fisherman there to give a clinic on how to be a better fisherman. All of this is done to bring customers into the stores and to make it fun. It gives customers a reason to want to go there versus anywhere else they could go to get comparably priced merchandise. It has become a big deal that is becoming more and more vendor driven than it is Wal-Mart driven.

One of the most important ways Sam Walton communicated his lofty service standards was through his unconditional product guarantees. In the Wal-Mart Visitor's Center in Bentonville,

Arkansas, is a four-sided glass display case containing actual merchandise returns Mr. Sam had accepted in the early days. One of
the items in the case is a great big round thermometer the kind
you can see from far away. The one in the glass case is old and
yellow and the numbers are so faded you can hardly read them.
The caption under the thermometer says the customer returned
this to Wal-Mart, stating it would no longer keep accurate tem-
peratures. Mr. Sam exchanged it for a new one. A second item in
the case is an old tennis racquet that someone had smashed
against the ground. The customer returned that racquet to Wal-
Mart, saying he could no longer serve tennis balls properly with
it. The notation says the customer was given a full refund. The
third item is a golf club. The golf club is shaped like a circle as if
someone had wrapped it around a tree. The description in the
case says Mr. Sam took this golf club back even though he knew
there was nothing wrong with it; it wasn't defective. The customer brought it back and at Wal-Mart our goal is no-hassle
returns. A final item in that case is a Stanley thermos bottle that
was completely rusted out. Stanley discontinued manufacturing
that thermos bottle 5 years before the first Wal-Mart store
opened. The customer brought the thermos back to Wal-Mart,
saying it would no longer keep hot things hot and was promptly
given a full refund. A store manager who worked with Sam
Walton told me the following story about his initial reaction to
Wal-Mart's product guarantees:

> Early on in my career working as an assistant manager for
> Wal-Mart, I had a really difficult time with Wal-Mart's prod-
> uct return policy. I grew up working in a small hardware store
> where merchandise returns would just kill you. Typically, if
> somebody brought something back to my granddad's hard-

ware store, it was up to the manufacturer to honor the warranty; our store didn't. So when I got to Wal-Mart, I saw Wal-Mart giving all this money away and I said I'm going to fix this problem. Wal-Mart's crazy, I'm going to help them straighten this out.

I learned very quickly from my first store manager about the refund policy at Wal-Mart. He said our refunds at Wal-Mart never, ever run more than 5 percent of our total sales. Half of that, or 2.5 percent, is merchandise that there is nothing at all wrong with that goes right back to the floor and we sell it at full retail. Of the other 2.5 percent, half of that, or 1.25 percent, has a slight damage or a defect and we have to take a small markdown on it and sell it as damaged goods. Of the other 1.25 percent, half of that, or 0.625 percent we send back to the vendor and get full credit on. That other 0.625 percent, the customer took us for and we absolutely have to eat it and we've lost it.

The point that he made to me which has remained with me for 18 years now, because I can still quote you these numbers is this: Are you really going to argue with a customer and potentially lose a customer for 0.625 percent? Let the people who are pulling the wool over our eyes leave here happy because they are going to come back here and they are going to shop with us and we're going to more than make up for that.

What is one of Wal-Mart's customers' worth to the store in terms of dollars spent? I estimate on average each customer spends somewhere in the neighborhood of $35.00 per week in a Wal-Mart store and if that customer visits the store once a week that represents over $1500 per year in purchases and over 10 years that purchase number might be $15,000. With the value of those purchases, why in the world would you want to risk losing a customer, because of a product return problem, who is worth that much to the company? The answer is you don't.

For this reason, Sam Walton put the service desk at the front of the store, when everybody else had theirs in the back corner. He did it to show every customer that came in that they could trust us. Buy anything here and if you don't like it or don't want it, bring it back and you're going to be taken care of. We believe in taking care of customers so strongly that we are going to do it up in front of all of the other shoppers so they can watch us take care of you. The service desk and the return policy at Wal-Mart is more of an advertising effort than it is anything else, at least it was for Mr. Sam. It was designed to advertise the fact that Wal-Mart will take care of you, don't go anywhere else, you don't need to because we'll take care of you! It's important to get across how to execute the return policy program to the people who are dealing with the customers day in and day out because this is the most powerful advertising you can possibly do for your store.

Mr. Sam's aggressive approach to service after the sale created a trust with his customers that made shopping his stores a no-risk proposition. His no-hassle, no-questions-asked return policy gives his loyal customers the feeling, Why shop anywhere else? He treated his customers like they were his neighbors and trusted friends. To this day Wal-Mart is rewarded each week of the year as millions and millions of loyal customers return again and again to shop in its stores.

Sam Walton had already developed standards for internal customer service long before others had even thought about it as a concept. Wal-Mart's leaders require its managers and associates to have the same high standards for serving their fellow associates that they use in serving their external customers in the stores. Mr. Sam realized that what gets measured in an organization is what gets done so he initiated the use of internal customer service evaluations to monitor the quality of service provided between individuals and departments. It was his way of positively impacting his internal and external service standards. These reviews were truly 360° allowing the company's associates to provide input on the performance of their own supervisors.

By setting high standards for service, intradepartmental and interdepartmental squabbling was minimized and replaced by a spirit of cooperation. The service level provided between and within departments at the Wal-Mart Home Office is unlike anything I have seen before or since in my experiences in other companies. When I worked there, all I had to do was ask and I'd get all the help I needed from other departments! I wouldn't hear a litany of excuses or reasons why the other department was so busy they couldn't possibly help; I never heard anyone at Wal-Mart say, "It's not my job." I think because of the merchant mentality Sam Walton instilled in the culture, everyone pitches in to help wherever they can. The team synergy resulting from the spirit of teamwork and cooperation of its people creates an incredible customer service competitive advantage for the company. Imagine the power of Mr. Sam's army of loyal associates working together to enthusiastically help one another to exceed the expectations of their customers!

CONTROL EXPENSES and
Save Your Way to Prosperity

Mr. Sam was proud of the tightfisted
persona created by Wal-Mart around
the world; cheap is chic at Wal-Mart!

S am Walton was the first to admit that he was cheap as the day is long. A store manager who met Mr. Sam many times said that when he visited his store, he never carried any money. As well off as he was, he rarely had a quarter or 50 cents in his pocket so he would always ask somebody if they'd buy him a soda. He was tightfisted when it came to spending money, and he was proud of it! He trained the rest of his team to think exactly the same way. He believed that one of the fast ways to drop big-time dollars to the bottom line was by either not spending money unnecessarily in the first place or by ferreting out cost savings in every conceivable area of his operation. Sam Walton was like the famous magician and illusionist Harry Houdini when it came to his ability to magically find ways to cut costs and save money. Ask Wal-Mart's competitors and they'll tell you it is no illusion that Wal-Mart has the lowest cost structure in the retailing industry; they'll also tell you that its expense structure is one of its most compelling competitive advantages in the marketplace. It is a fact that Sam Walton controlled his expenses better than any of his competitors, but the thing that is really extraordinary is how he got everyone else in his company to think and act like tightwads too!

Sam Walton's ninth success secret for achieving remarkable results is, *"CONTROL EXPENSES and save your way to prosperity."* Whoever said, "You can't save your way to prosperity," never met Sam Walton, the king of cost savings. He grew up during the Depression years and his mother and father taught him their approach to money, which was to save it rather than spend it. He carried that lesson with him into adulthood. He had figured out in the early days of his business, as every entrepreneur discovers out of necessity, that frugality is a virtue. With so many stores, distribution centers, and products, the endless pursuit of reducing waste and needless expenditures wrings incredible bottom-line cost savings out of his company. Look at it this way: With sales approaching $300 billion, a 1 percent saving as a percentage of total sales represents $3 billion to Wal-Mart's bottom line! Trust me when I tell you that's exactly what company leaders try to do to create additional profitability. Wal-Mart's leaders simultaneously juggle the growth of top-line sales as they focus simultaneously on running as efficient an operation as possible. Mr. Sam believed that if competitors were efficient in managing their own expenses, they'd have an excellent chance of surviving the onslaught of the highly efficient "big box" retailers.

When he first started opening stores, Sam Walton hired many experienced small business owners who had the same entrepreneurial mindset that he had. Having run a business, they were used to tightly managing expenses and he liked that because they were as cheap as he was. Owners know the importance of managing money and what it takes to make the payroll and pay the bills each month. They spend money carefully, budgeting their scarce resources one day at a time. Mr. Sam liked people who understood the value of a dollar and who wouldn't think of spending money foolishly. Someone shared an acronym with me: CHEAP that captures the critical attributes of founding entrepreneurs, business owners, and effective business leaders, which are Committed, Honest, Executes, Able, and Performs. When I first heard this acronym, the first person I thought of was Sam Walton. I am certain that had Sam Walton discovered it, he would have adopted CHEAP as a Wal-Mart mantra to teach the attributes of the entrepreneur to everyone in a fun and humorous way, but with the serious goal of reinforcing the importance of saving money.

I hope you are getting the point that Sam Walton was proud of his reputation as a penny-pincher and that he instilled the same zeal for thrift in his associates. The result of everyone's enthusiasm for controlling expenses is that expenses as a percentage of sales at Wal-Mart run significantly lower than at any of its competitors. This in turn creates a major pricing advantage for Wal-Mart that enables the company to sell its merchandise at much lower prices than any one else while still maintaining strong profit margins. You see, Mr. Sam believed in passing cost savings along to the customer in the form of lower prices. The combination of high sales per square foot (which continue to grow every year) and constant pressure to maintain or reduce costs makes Wal-Mart the most productive company in retailing. Company leaders are proud of their reputation for being tight with a buck; being cheap really is chic if you work at Wal-Mart!

Sam Walton's merchandise buying team is renowned in manufacturing circles for their ability to demand the lowest possible purchase prices for good-quality products. He required that his buyers operate with integrity, and they were not allowed to accept gratuities even as small as a free baseball cap from a vendor. When I worked there, I remember I was told that I must pay for my own meals even when others who didn't work for the company offered to buy me dinner. This standard created arm's-length relationships with Wal-Mart's suppliers, adding objectivity and a bit of additional tension to every negotiation. Suppliers who were used to using sales ploys to soften up their customers were forced to deal straight up on price when dealing with Wal-Mart. Game playing, positioning, and posturing were not only frowned upon but would likely lead to no business for that manufacturer or supplier. For many manufacturers and suppliers this standard necessitated changing the way they did business.

Manufacturers and suppliers weren't used to retailers controlling the purchasing negotiations the way Sam Walton did. The only choice you have when you deal with Wal-Mart is to deliver your products at the specified price or you can choose not to supply their stores. That's not to say Mr. Sam was unfair in his dealings. He expected his suppliers to make a fair profit but no more. In order to get their operations efficient enough to provide products to Wal-Mart at the lowest possible prices and still eke out a profit, many manufacturers have had to change the way they do business. Some have moved their operations offshore in order to lower their cost structures. Others have continued to manufacture domestically, accepting lower margins, or may actually break even or even lose money supplying Wal-Mart, making up margin shortfalls elsewhere. Still other manufacturers have chosen not to supply Wal-Mart altogether due to their inability to achieve the efficiencies required to make enough profit to justify the effort to supply its stores. It seems supplying the retail giant is the dream of many manufacturers. For some when that dream comes true, they may later find it becomes a nightmare when they figure out they can't supply their products profitably without changing the way they do business.

I talked to one of Wal-Mart's vendors and he explained to me an interesting way Wal-Mart saves money when it purchases products from manufacturers and suppliers:

> When we ship products to Wal-Mart we invoice them through electronic data interchange (EDI) and in 60 days we get our check. The underlying strategy for Wal-Mart with respect to selling products is to receive products and to sell them to customers before they even have a chance to pay the vendors for them. If your product is turning over six times per year, they are doing that or you are right on the money. If you're getting more than six turns a year, then you are ahead of the ballgame. When that happens, Wal-Mart has received and sold your product before they even cut you a check for it.

In order to keep the big-brand manufacturers honest in their dealings with Wal-Mart, Mr. Sam manufactured his own line of private-label products. His private-label line was designed to offer lower-priced product alternatives for his customers at comparable quality to the big brands. The products are cheaper and the margins are higher; by producing them himself, he lowered his own expenses. At last count over 1,600 products in Wal-Mart's stores are generated under the Great Value private-label line. Creating generic versions of existing brands by knocking them off at an equal or higher-quality level provides Wal-Mart's price-conscious shoppers with an alternative choice of products offering real value. Wal-Mart controls the quality of the products because it controls the product development and the manufacturing of those products. Teams of Wal-Mart associates are dedicated to the development of the Great Value line of products. So it turns out Wal-Mart isn't just a retailer of the products manufactured by others; it is also a major manufacturer of products. Offering private-label and generic products fits nicely into Wal-Mart's everyday low-price philosophy. The company also lowers its own expenses when it sells its own products. Even though the products are sold at considerably lower prices, the margins are much higher, dropping dollars to the bottom line. A merchandise buyer who worked with Sam Walton shared this story about the impact of private-label products on the consumer, branded product manufacturers, and the company:

> Why do you think private-label products are out there in the first place? Why does someone buy generic pharmaceuticals versus branded? It's because the customer is going to save money. Wal-Mart went into private-label products in order to give the customer a better value. Generic products and private-label products put a lot of pressure on branded product

manufacturers so they don't think there is receptivity to raising the prices on their brands. If you don't have any competition, obviously prices will go up. So Wal-Mart's private label worked a couple of different ways: first, to stifle the branded merchandise, and second, to offer a better value to the customer. Offering generic merchandise keeps the brands honest and from Wal-Mart's perspective its own private label products offer higher margins.

A good example of a branded versus a private-label product is Pam Non-Stick Cooking Spray versus Wal-Mart's Great Value, No Stick Cooking Spray. From a quality standpoint, the two products are exactly the same. From a price standpoint, the Great Value product offers much better value to the customer. When Wal-Mart creates its own Great Value private-label products it uses its own testing labs to develop products that are equal to or exceed the original product that they are knocking off. When you go into the pharmacy area at Wal-Mart, look for Sudafed and you'll find Wal-Mart's private-label Sudafed right next to the original brand. You can be assured that the quality of the private-label version is exactly the same or better than the branded merchandise although you'll pay much less for the private label. Most people don't know this fact. When I go to Wal-Mart, I know when I buy their private label I am saving money, but I'm also buying the same exact same thing that the brands offer. I'm not giving the branded manufacturer my money for their advertising when I can get the same quality of product or better buying private label. The products are tested extensively before a product ever comes to market. The value created for customers by offering private-label brands, coupled with the higher margins generated for the company, is yet another way Sam Walton figured out how to increase sales, improve profitability, and lower his expenses.

With a company the size of Wal-Mart, seemingly small cost savings can make a huge difference. Sam Walton designed a way to culturally communicate the importance of cost saving ideas called "Yes we can Sam." Through this program all associates are encouraged to come up with cost saving ideas at a local level to lower the cost of doing business. The kinds of ideas Mr. Sam was looking for from his associates were ways to save $5, $10, $20, $50, or $100, and he knew that every once in a while someone would come up with a whale of an idea to save big bucks. Once the best cost saving ideas were identified, he could easily replicate them across the entire chain of stores. A $100 cost saving idea at one store is worth $700,000 when it is implemented across a chain of 7,000 stores! Ideas that were deemed successful were recognized by the district manager and store manager, and the associate received a great job pin. Four great job pins could be exchanged for one share of Wal-Mart stock. However, the big motivation on the part of Mr. Sam's associates to improve Wal-Mart's operations was in order to improve their own chances of receiving profit sharing and a store stakeholder's bonus check at the end of the year.

The chance to influence their own profit sharing turned Wal-Mart's associates into a highly motivated and focused team of cost busters. Cutting and controlling expenses is one of the areas associates could directly impact every day to substantially impact bottom-line financial results. Wal-Mart's army of associates even believed they could directly impact the value of the company's stock. By taking responsibility and ownership for managing expenses, Mr. Sam's associates took thriftiness to a whole new level. I can still remember the associates working around me policing the wasteful practices of themselves and those around them. The associates were encouraged to confront the wasteful practices of their fellow associates and even those of their managers!

Because of profit sharing Mr. Sam was able to culturally integrate cost control to the point where his associates were obsessed with saving the company's way to prosperity! The associates worried about saving the company money as much as the company leaders did. It got to the point that associates were willing to do whatever it took cut company costs, including taking it upon themselves to decide to bring their personal office supplies from home for use in their jobs at the company. I saw it happening every day in my own department. The associates brought the basic office necessities from their homes to outfit their desks, including pens, pencils, staplers, staples, paper clips, Post-It notes, rubber bands, high-lighter pens, tape, and calculators. I can assure you that no one in management told them to do this; it was something the associates themselves reinforced culturally. When I asked associates the reason behind bringing supplies from home I was told it was their contribution to saving the company money in order to directly impact their own profit sharing.

I know as you're reading this you're thinking that's impossible or that didn't happen. I'm here to tell you it did happen, and it happened all around the company. I found myself bringing my personal office supplies from home to do my part to help lower company costs. The associates recycle everything, including paper-clips and rubber bands. The idea is if you sweat the small stuff by worrying about the pennies, nickels, and dimes, the waste of big-time dollars just won't happen.

Mr. Sam and the other executives were just as focused as everyone else on doing their part to keep costs under control. They traveled coach class on commercial flights, ate at cafeteria-style restaurants, and even stayed two to a room at budget hotels to reduce costs. Here's a story a store manager shared with me about a memorable luncheon meeting he had with Sam Walton when Mr. Sam visited his Wal-Mart Discount Store:

> At about 11:30 Mr. Sam said to all the managers, "I'm getting a little hungry, ya'll want to go eat?" He said, "I'm going to go over to the food department and get some saltine crackers and I'll meet you in the break room. Ya'll go get whatever you want to eat." So that's where we had lunch, in the break room with him eating saltine crackers and us eating whatever we could scrounge (and pay for) out of the food department for a lunch break! We talked business the whole time we were "at lunch."

Wal-Mart's executives didn't have country club memberships, company cars, or even private parking spaces. Their offices were inexpensively outfitted, and the building they were in was a converted warehouse. Even the coffee they drank in their offices at the headquarters wasn't free! They believed in leading by example. Mr. Sam said, "How can we as leaders expect the associates to listen to our cost control message if the executives are saying one thing and doing another?" The answer is you can't!

The first time I did my departmental budget, I asked about how to budget for overtime. I was told every department, every store, and every distribution center had the same budget for overtime, but unfortunately that budget had zero dollars in it. Mr. Sam believed that paying overtime was a waste of money because you increased your labor costs by 50 percent or more when you paid time-and-a-half. When I asked who would do the work that didn't get done when the hourly paid associates went home, I was told that salaried managers were free to work as many hours as they needed to get it done. In fact all of the managers work a 5½- to 6-day work week, including those who work at the home office. Managers with no overtime budget to fall back upon get very good at managing their hourly paid staff efficiently to get the work done within the straight-time hours allotted.

I was also told I couldn't add any staff even though we were opening stores at a frenetic pace, increasing the work loads of everyone supporting the stores. I was told not to worry about the work load until the staff was so overwhelmed that "the pig squealed"; at that point we'd take a look at staffing levels, but only then! Interestingly enough, I noticed that the existing staff accepted the fact that no additional staff would be added without complaint and simply worked harder to get the increased workload done.

Expense control was communicated to everyone uniformly as part of the company's total quality effort. Mr. Sam's vendor partners at companies like Procter & Gamble and GE shared all of their best quality practices with Wal-Mart. One of the pillars of quality at Wal-Mart was cost control. Training was provided to all home office associates in flow-charting processes to identify opportunities to improve efficiency by reducing steps, thus reducing the time to complete complex and simple activities. I was mesmerized by the improved process solutions that groups of hourly paid associates came up with to save the company time and money. The associates were empowered to identify any process in need of improvement and were given the time to meet to put together a plan of action. Every area of the operation was fair game, and there were no processes immune from scrutiny. Some of the savings identified resulted in cutting time out of existing procedures by eliminating unnecessary steps, forms, or signoffs. Seeing associates solving real tough business problems without management involvement was refreshing. This is what empowerment of employees is supposed to accomplish.

Empowered associates were taught to negotiate everything on behalf of the company. Every vendor, every ongoing supply need, and every new purchase was negotiated by the associates in the same manner as they might do comparison shopping when they bought things for their homes. They didn't care what the advertised price for an item was, and they didn't care what every other company paid for a product or service; they expected and demanded a much lower Wal-Mart price on everything purchased. The way they got that price was by pitting local vendors against one another every time they made a purchase, using the same techniques each of them would use to do comparison shopping for personal purchases. It worked extremely well, with suppliers providing discounts on everything you can imagine.

One example of this negotiation technique involved one of our existing vendors who supplied drug screening services, for our drug testing program of potential new employees at stores across the United States. This was a multimillion dollar contract with a well-known laboratory company. We tested hundreds of thousands of applicants for jobs as part of our drug-free workplace policy, with our vendor providing testing services at its headquarters in the Carolinas. Because of the urgency to fill jobs, we needed to get drug screening results turned around as quickly as possible. Using total quality flow charting, we figured out we could reduce the turnaround time of drug testing results by working with a new drug screening laboratory strategically located in Memphis, Tennessee, the hub for Federal Express. We visited our proposed vendor and we visited Federal Express while we were in Memphis to work out the logistics of faster testing. FedEx agreed to let our vendor pick up their own packages as they arrived in Memphis in the middle of the night, allowing lab employees to test samples in the wee hours of the morning. Thus, results could be electronically transmitted to the home office drug screening department and the results could be released to stores first thing in the morning. The previous procedure took an additional 24 hours to turn results around as the drug testing company had to wait for samples to arrive in the Carolinas before they could be tested. The bottom line was the new vendor could get us quality results faster and at a lower price.

When our current vendor was told of our decision in a phone call about why we had made the decision, the company president asked if he could come to Bentonville to discuss alternatives before we gave the contract to the other service provider. Our current drug screening provider agreed to provide upgraded computer systems, less expensive testing, and an onsite drug results supervisor at the Wal-Mart home office (paid for by his company), and even agreed to open a laboratory in Memphis to service the drug screening needs of Wal-Mart. We even got them to give us a price concession on the cost of testing each sample. He exceeded our expectations so we let his company keep the business. This is just one example of how far Wal-Mart's associates are willing to go to make certain everything they purchase is at the lowest possible price.

When we traveled we always got the lowest-cost flights, rental cars, and hotel rooms. Everything was negotiated by the Wal-Mart travel department on our behalf. It wasn't unusual to get ticketed on a low-cost commercial flight requiring two or more connections to a final destination. When I worked for other *Fortune* 500 companies, we almost always paid inflated prices for airline tickets and no one seemed to care. I noticed over the years that people who work for organizations seem to have a double standard when it comes to spending money. Many will spend the organization's money on an expensive round-trip airline ticket without any concern for the cost, but when they travel on a personal vacation they go to great lengths to get the lowest possible cost. Mr. Sam expected everyone to negotiate as if they were writing the check out of their personal checking account.

I run my own business using the lessons I learned at Wal-Mart when I travel to this day. On a recent trip I did it the Wal-Mart way. I was attending a business meeting in Reno, Nevada, and I was quoted $1400 for a round-trip ticket for a direct flight from Pittsburgh, Pennsylvania, to Reno, Nevada. I checked flights out of Cleveland, Ohio (which is a 2-hour drive from my home), on Southwest Airlines and I found a flight for $204 round trip! The catch was I had to connect through Kansas City, Las Vegas, and then on to Reno. Since I was spending my own money and I controlled my own schedule, I took the Cleveland flight and saved myself almost $1200. When I go to New York, I fly on a discount airline for $150 round trip, connecting through Washington Dulles, rather than pay up to $600 for a direct flight on another airline. I have to get up earlier and it takes more time, but the savings are substantial. I stay out near the Newark Airport in a room that costs less than $100 per night versus $300 or more per night in Manhattan. For about $10 I take a train rather than a $50 cab ride into the city in time for meetings which never start before 9:00 A.M. That's the Wal-Mart way.

Imagine how much money Wal-Mart saves by using this common-sense cost-saving idea with as many people traveling as they have! Try to implement a simple cost-saving idea like this one at your own organization and you'll hear a litany of excuses from people who will tell you they are too busy to waste their personal time sitting in airports or riding trains. I always find I get quality, uninterrupted work done every time I travel using this technique, and I feel good about traveling because I know I am saving money.

Imagine the possibilities of almost 2 million associates empowered and focused on sales, service, and controlling waste! I saw some simple commonsense examples of expense control that were embraced across Wal-Mart that saved lots of money. At one of the Saturday morning meetings Mr. Sam brought in an example of the ingenuity of one of the information technology associates who had asked Mr. Sam the question, "Why are we wasting paper?" The associate had told Sam Walton that he hauled a large cart load of computer reports (hundreds of pounds) to several different departments each week and after he dropped them off he'd pick up the same-size stack of old reports to be discarded from the previous week. He'd been doing this exercise for a long time and he had come to the conclusion that the amount of associates actually using the reports wasn't justifying the cost of producing them and the cost of all that paper. He decided to take it upon himself to question the waste of time, effort, and paper so he personally took the initiative to bring this situation to Mr. Sam's attention.

In a theatrical fashion Sam Walton had the associate roll the cart of paper into the Saturday morning meeting as a visible example of wasteful practices. He had the associate explain the same story he had told Mr. Sam of what he had found in his own words for everyone in attendance to hear. I'll never forget the visual impact of seeing that example of waste and hearing the story behind it. Of course, it was agreed that the reports would be eliminated immediately, saving the company a great deal of money on an annual basis. As it turns out those reports had served a purpose at some point in time, but that purpose was long gone. This is a great example of the kind of grassroots cost control effort he wanted to see replicated by associates everywhere.

The penny-pinching mentality was driven by Sam Walton himself, but the effort by associates to contribute to their own profit sharing is truly grassroots. The effort by associates to help the company have the lowest costs in the industry is truly extraordinary. Try this simple example of the Wal-Mart way in your organization to test your culture's receptivity to controlling costs. Ask everyone to use the back side of every piece of paper before they throw it out or better yet recycle it. Mr. Sam instituted the practice of using paper on both sides, which reduces paper costs by 50 percent! The savings are substantial, but even this simple example is almost impossible for many organizations to replicate due to cultural resistance to change.

At Wal-Mart and in your organization, cost control is a team effort. Everyone must focus constantly on reducing costs in the tireless and endless pursuit of finding ways to control and cut operational expenses. The real trick is finding ways to reduce expenses while simultaneously continuing to operate the business efficiently and effectively. To accomplish this goal, Wal-Mart's employees and yours, at all levels, can assist in providing suggestions and ideas for operational cost reductions in every area of the business. It's the people who are closest to the work and closest to the customer who have the best ideas. The benefits of such programs include promoting teamwork, improving morale, and recognition of the good ideas of employees. Some companies view the contributions of their employees as so critical to reducing and controlling costs that they have even developed formalized cost buster programs. Wal-Mart's program, called "Yes We Can Sam," was designed to provide recognition to the associates who provide good cost-saving ideas that could be implemented.

There is an endless list of cost-saving areas over which your employees have some direct control, including elimination of archaic procedures, reducing overtime, consulting fees, travel expenses, employment advertising, memberships, dues, electricity, heat, and air conditioning, the use of technology to eliminate manual work, and even outsourcing work.

The cultural integration of cost savings as a pillar of total quality has made expense control a core competency at Wal-Mart.

Managing costs creates as much impact on Wal-Mart's low-price strategy as their ability to leverage their economies of scale in purchasing their merchandise originally. Said another way, Wal-Mart is not only able to purchase merchandise at prices below what its competitors can, but its total cost structure in every area of the business as a percentage of sales is also lower. The company's profits are derived through a combination of tough buyer negotiations on the front end and the company's constant focus on controlling or reducing costs. The goal is to get associates to identify and eliminate costs in every area. Product costs are also reduced by tirelessly working with its manufacturers to increase their efficiency so that those cost savings will allow Wal-Mart to purchase at the lowest possible prices. Wal-Mart passes any reductions in its cost of purchasing along to customers by lowering its retail prices, putting competitors in a position where they can't compete on price. Therein lies the real competitive success story of Wal-Mart; its purchasing power coupled with Mr. Sam's never-ending quest for lower expenses were like a double whammy for his competitors!

SWIM UPSTREAM, Be Different, and Challenge the Status Quo

Sam Walton was the first to admit that many of the risks he took ended in failure, but he believed if only 1 or 2 out of 10 of those risks succeeded, it made dealing with all those other failures worthwhile!

S am Walton has always talked about being the best retailer in the world; his goal was never to be the biggest. Imagine the challenges he faced, and that he had to overcome along the way, as he built a business model that had never been tried before. When you take into account the sheer size of his stores, the number of suppliers, the number of employees, and the geographic dispersion of the company, you begin to sense the weighty challenges he overcame. He garnered huge shares of mature markets and products by leveraging Wal-Mart's massive economies of scale. With no examples to follow or copy he was forced to develop his own ideas and solutions to problems, and he was forced to develop those solutions while he ran his rapidly growing company. Like a train roaring down the tracks at breakneck speed, Mr. Sam and his associates were frantically out in front laying track as quickly as they could to keep the Wal-Mart train rolling to yet-to-be-determined destinations.

Circumstances forced Sam Walton to be different and to swim upstream, and because of his unique approach he intentionally and admittedly broke many of the conventional rules for how things were to be done. Along the way in his quest to succeed, he challenged many of the existing leadership and business paradigms. While Mr. Sam was out innovating in rural America, others didn't take him seriously enough to imitate his trailblazing practices. His competitors continued down the tried and true path, seemingly unaware that competition as they had always known it had changed forever. Competitive strategies that they had used that had always worked for them in the past weren't going to work any longer as a result of Mr. Sam challenging the status quo. Unfortunately, many of those competitors failed because they were unable to change direction even when they finally figured out the error of their ways.

It's truly amazing what Wal-Mart has accomplished and the way Sam Walton orchestrated it all was by challenging the conventional wisdom and taking risks. Sam Walton's tenth success secret for achieving remarkable results is, "*SWIM UPSTREAM, be different, and challenge the status quo.*" He believed in blazing his own trails by challenging the tried and true ways of doing things. Mr. Sam said, "If everyone else is doing it this way, why don't we try doing the same thing in an unconventional way?" He believed that by taking that approach, you could often find the competitive advantage. What he often found was that the tried and true path was the path of least resistance; it was conventional and it was easy.

His trailblazing practices were often more difficult to implement and often that was because everyone else he was forced to work with outside his company kept trying to cling to what they already knew. His biggest challenge often was overcoming resistance to change. It was as if everyone else he encountered in the industry was interested in comfortably picking the lowest hanging fruit within easy reach while Sam Walton wanted to climb the tree and reach for the most inaccessible fruit on the highest branches. In the process of swimming upstream and ignoring the conventional wisdom, he changed the way the world of business is conducted by forcing his competitors, his manufacturers, and his suppliers to change or face extinction. The biggest benefactor of his visionary strategies is the consumer of products around the world.

More often than not people who are confronted with problems in life take the well worn path in search of traditional or conventional solutions. Not Sam Walton. Whenever Mr. Sam faced a challenge or a problem, he viewed it as an opportunity; you might say he looked for the silver lining in every cloud. He had a knack for discovering new, sometimes radical, and less expensive ways of accomplishing his goals. He even had a term for his challenges to the status quo; he called it "swimming upstream." When faced with obstacles, people have a tendency in life to seek the solutions that are most commonly used to solve a problem. In most cases this is a good way to come up with a satisfactory solution. Sometimes by searching for a unique way of resolving a problem, an even better outcome can be found. This is how Sam Walton believed you can find the competitive advantage in life.

Sam Walton taught the people around him to take calculated risks and try new ways of doing things. He was the first to admit that 9 out of 10 times his trailblazing into new directions may not have worked, but it was that tenth time when it did work that Mr. Sam believed made it all worthwhile. Others might view so many failures as a waste of time, energy, and effort, but not Sam Walton. He learned valuable lessons from each of his business experiments, and it's those lessons that led to big breakthrough strategies later on. Those early research and development efforts form the foundation of many of Wal-Mart's best business practices to this day. All of us can learn a valuable lesson from Sam Walton about overcoming adversity and achieving success by simply learning from our inevitable mistakes and failures along the way. They call that experience and in life both our good and bad experiences are ultimately our best teacher.

One of Wal-Mart's store managers put it best when he described swimming upstream as, "Get out of the box, be aggressive, be a maverick, and don't let people tell you that you can and can't do." That's exactly what Sam Walton had to do in his personal swim upstream when he started Wal-Mart. In establishing his rural retailing strategy, he was challenging the existing paradigms in retail. Along the way, he had more than his share of critics and business fortune tellers who were more than happy to predict the future demise of his enterprise. But Mr. Sam remained steadfast in his quest to achieve his dream of building his business in rural America, and his success has been nothing short of astounding. He did it by always making his first priority the customer.

The story of Sam Walton, the entrepreneur, swimming upstream is the story of the epic struggles he faced to make Wal-Mart successful in the early and difficult days. There were plenty of bankers, suppliers, and competitors who said his trailblazing ideas wouldn't work. He was the first to admit that he made mistakes along the way; many of the ideas he tried didn't work, but some of them obviously did. So he tried and he failed, and he tried and he failed, and he tried again. In the end, Mr. Sam's radical way of approaching product purchasing, technology, and distribution has revolutionized the retailing industry.

What was it about his personality and leadership style that set Sam Walton apart? What did he do to "be different and challenge the status quo?" What made his approach so revolutionary? Why hadn't anyone else already challenged the existing customer service, manufacturing, and supplier paradigms? Why was he the right man, in the right place, at the right time? Was his success a result of destiny, vision, or luck? What lessons can everyone else learn from the world's most successful entrepreneur? I thought the best way to illustrate Mr. Sam's concept of swimming upstream and to answer these questions was by using examples of his actual trailblazing accomplishments. These are things he came up with and implemented himself that illustrate how he swam upstream. Interestingly enough, his challenges to the status quo crossed into every area of Wal-Mart's business including best practice strategies and tactics in price, operations, associate relations, culture, vendor relationships, product selection, expenses, talent, service, technology, and distribution/fleet logistics. Here are some exam-

ples of swimming upstream that others can learn from and duplicate in any organization. These are examples of areas where Sam
Walton and Wal-Mart have challenged conventional thinking and
taken risks:

- Simplify everything
- Technology
- Associate partnership
- Meet with associates
- Open-door policy
- Vendor partnerships
- RFID
- Pricing
- Advertising
- Merchandising
- Product inventory
- New store concepts

I'll cover each of these examples with my own insider's perspective as well as with insights provided by Wal-Mart's actual
store managers, buyers, and suppliers who knew and worked with
Sam Walton to help you understand how he swam upstream.

Simplify Everything

When I worked in the Wal-Mart headquarters, I remember Sam
Walton saying it was important for the leaders in the home office
to think about the people who would have to implement our
good ideas in the Wal-Mart Stores, Sam's Clubs and Distribution
Centers. If an idea couldn't be explained on one sheet of paper, it
was too complicated. In a company the size of Wal-Mart it's easy
to understand how even the simplest things can be difficult to

execute; that's why anything that was deemed complicated was destined to fail. Here's how a store manager describes the simplification process Mr. Sam came up with called, "one store at a time, one department at a time, one customer at a time:

> It simply means breaking down your business to the fundamentals and not getting so involved in thinking you are running a big company. The perception people have is that Wal-Mart is this big company up in Bentonville, but it is not; it is a collection of individual stores that just happens to have a home office in Bentonville, Arkansas. Every store is run as its own individual entity. That is broken down further by allowing each assistant manager to run his or her own area as if it were his or her own store by giving responsibility for payroll, staffing, inventory, merchandising, in-stock, mark-downs, and sales. Then you break it down further to the department manager level, and you let them run their own department as if it were a store by letting them monitor their sales and in stock every day and empowering them to affect those things. So basically, what you are doing is driving everything down. Ultimately, it comes down to focusing on dealing with that customer in front of you and not worrying about the 40,000 customers who are going to be coming into the store next week, because it's the customer in front of you who matters the most right now.

One of Sam Walton's most important beliefs was the simplification of everything the company did. He realized from his own experience that 90 percent of any strategy is the tactical execution of it. He knew that Wal-Mart's leaders, like most organization leaders, have a tendency to overly complicate solutions to business problems if they are given the chance. Other organizations teach people to "think big, start small, and scale up," whereas Wal-Mart thinks small, starts small, and then scales up." Sam Walton

believed it is easier to develop complex, hard-to-implement strategies than it is to design solutions that are simple and easy to execute. He also believed that professionally trained managers have a
tendency to unnecessarily overcomplicate things. Embracing the
KISS (Keep It Simple Stupid) concept and simplifying everything
you do are lessons all of us should steal shamelessly from Sam
Walton and implement now!

Technology

One of the best examples of Sam Walton's commitment to the success of Wal-Mart was the investment he was willing to make in
technology. Being tight with a buck, Mr. Sam hated the idea of
spending so much money on technology, but he loved the results
the company received from investing in it. As a result of investing
in systems, his company has become one of the most technologi-
cally advanced companies in the world; in fact, the only technological systems larger than Wal-Mart's are those belonging to the
federal government at the Pentagon. Customers would never sus-
pect the company's commitment to technology when they walk
into a Wal-Mart and are greeted by one of its friendly and folksy
associates. Wal-Mart's supply chain is completely driven by state-
of-the-art technology. Professors at business schools around the
world use Wal-Mart's technology as a case study for teaching their
students. Branches of our own federal government have met with
Wal-Mart's technology gurus and supply chain experts to learn
their best-practice strategies and tactics. One store manager offered
his perspective on the importance of Wal-Mart's commitment to
technology to the success of the company:

> The way that Sam Walton invested very heavily in technology
> is a good example of swimming upstream. Wal-Mart was one

of the first national retailers to put in scanning. When other retailers were just worried about the fundamentals and the basics like ticketing the merchandise and putting it on the floor, Wal-Mart invested in technology because Mr. Sam had a vision that down the road more information was going to help fine-tune their business. Initially, Mr. Sam was laughed at and ridiculed for the investment he had made in technology, which everyone now knows has paid back dividends a thousand times over. That's the biggest thing that set Wal-Mart apart back in the early days.

The beauty of many of Wal-Mart's technological advances, from a competitive perspective, is the fact that many of its competitors are unable to take advantage of the same technologies. The cost savings associated with technological advances are passed along to customers in the form of lower prices.

Associate Partnership

Sam Walton really believed in treating all of his associates like true business partners, like business associates. One of the ways he proved his sincerity was by opening the books and showing all of the associates the company's financial results. This was an unheard-of practice when Mr. Sam started doing it. Most leaders at other companies view their company's detailed financial reports as confidential. Sam Walton viewed the downside of competitors getting a look at his numbers as a small problem compared to the tremendous upside benefits of associates knowing what was going on so that they could help improve the business on an ongoing basis. Here is an insight shared with me by a Wal-Mart store manager:

> The way Wal-Mart shares numbers with its associates is a great example of Mr. Sam's swimming upstream philosophy. Virtually every associate who works in the stores has complete

access to the profit and loss statement. I don't know if any other company out there, even today, that shares that kind of intimate knowledge with their people. Wal-Mart's philosophy was if we share the information with you then you can help us make the best decisions so we're going to treat you like a partner. It was revolutionary when it was first introduced and it is still one of the things that sets Wal-Mart apart to this day. You can't just call somebody a partner; you have to really get them involved and treat them like one.

Meet with Associates

Mr. Sam required his store and distribution center managers to meet with the associates each and every day. That's how much he valued the importance of keeping people informed. In the locations that are open twenty-four hours a day, this meant holding one meeting with the associates on each of the three shifts. This was just one of the many ways he treated the associates like business partners. A store manager described these meetings for me:

> Daily you are required to have what is called your 10-minute meeting. They last a lot longer than 10 minutes but initially it was designed to be a 10-minute meeting. You cover the priorities and the numbers quickly and you recognize a few people and you do that with every shift. These 10-minute meetings keep everyone involved with what is going on by sharing information and priorities and you recognize top performers. Then weekly you have other meetings like a loss prevention meeting and a department manager meeting. The store manager participates in these department manager meetings by discussing priorities, issues, and merchandising plans. Assistant managers meet with their department managers every day.
>
> Also, annually, after the store manager attends the January year beginning meeting, a series of mandatory meetings are

held at every store, covering all associates. All of the information the store manager learned at the year beginning meeting, like new concepts and new policies, is reviewed. Also, a discussion is held with the associates concerning what the associates feel are the top issues in their store and a store plan is developed for the coming year.

The associates are kept informed of progress toward company goals, and they are asked for input to improve the operation. Wal-Mart's two way communication with its associates is one of its more important competitive advantages.

Open-Door Policy

If I had to point to the most important reason why Wal-Mart's operations have remained nonunion, it would be because of the open-door policy. Allowing any associate to gain access to higher levels of management in order to resolve concerns eliminates the perceived need by associates for third-party intervention. However, that's not the reason Sam Walton created the open-door policy. Mr. Sam implemented the open-door policy because of his belief in the Golden Rule. He believed his managers should treat the associates the way they themselves would want to be treated. One of his store managers explained the open-door policy this way:

> The open door, simply put, allows associates to take any concern to any level of management they wish to. Associates are asked to give their supervisor (or their supervisor, if the supervisor is the issue) the opportunity to correct the issue, but that is not a requirement. It goes back to the grassroots nature of the company to address issues from a level as close to the problem as possible. Once the associate has taken their concern to a level of management, and if they did not receive a satisfactory response, they were welcome to continue on to the

next step in the chain of communication, and so on and so on, all the way to the company president. Understanding, of course, that they may not ever receive the answer they want to hear. The charge from Mr. Sam was to always try to find a resolution that favored the associate, if at all possible.

From a practical standpoint, the open-door issues usually were not addressed by the department manager (more often this is where the issue began). Even assistant managers are handling fewer open-door issues as the company grows and we continue to have less and less experienced individuals becoming assistant managers. Co-managers addressed most open door issues, with the store manager handling the more serious concerns. Often though, because as a store manager you are out walking the floor and talking with associates, the issues come to you first. Whenever that happened to me I would typically bring the assistant manager (once I had determined the assistant was not the issue) in along with the associate and discuss the issue. Then, in front of the associate, I would ask the assistant manager to address the issues and get back to me on how it was resolved. This gave the associate the feeling of having the boss involved, but freed me up from actually having to go out and correct the issue. Then, always, I would follow up later with the associate and verify the issue was handled appropriately.

The district manager would often be the first to get a phone call, but typically it fell back to the store manager to then correct the issue with the district manager doing the "warm and fuzzy" by following up with the associate on their next visit to the store. HR (People Division) would only get involved in the larger issues (harassment, discrimination, etc.), or if a particular store was having an excess amount of open-door issues.

The concern Sam Walton showed for his associates is legendary within Wal-Mart and his open-door policy remains one of the basic operating principles of the company to this day.

Vendor Partnerships

Sam Walton's extraordinary vision for Wal-Mart was built upon an integrity-based relationship with his suppliers, his associates, and his customers. As Wal-Mart grew larger and technology became more critical, vendor partnerships were necessary in order to manage the supply chain efficiently. With over 100,000 SKUs (stock keeping units) and thousands of stores, vendor management of inventory was the only way Wal-Mart could efficiently keep its shelves in stock. Mr. Sam brought his suppliers in as business partners and both were focused on selling products at retail. One of Wal-Mart's vendors described vendor partnerships this way:

> Wal-Mart was the first retailer to make its vendors true business partners. Wal-Mart opened a store in Kentucky that was completely vendor-managed, where the vendors got to come in and set their own planograms. They were told, this is how much space you are allocated and you merchandise the way that you think you can get the best return on your merchandise for yourself; be greedy. They were told to put the merchandise, the number of SKUs, and the assortment in that store that they thought would sell the most.
>
> That was the pilot test for making the vendors "partners with the company" and having an input on what the assortment is in the stores, and how many pieces stay on the shelf at a time to maximize inventory turns. This idea led to a different way of thinking. Most retailers have to be wary of their vendors because if they are not careful, the vendor will really overstock the store just to get a sale. At Wal-Mart, and I can tell you from being one of their vendors, you don't have that mentality.
>
> You are constantly trying to figure out how you can improve the business for Wal-Mart, because if I improve it for

Wal-Mart, I'll improve it for me. The partnership between vendors and Wal-Mart ties the vendor's future into making Wal-Mart a success. The focus of that partnership is in how to make Wal-Mart a success, rather then how do I make my company a success, which is a little bit of a paradigm shift for those who aren't familiar with this. Most vendors are out there just trying to get the big sale for their own benefit.

As a Wal-Mart vendor I can tell you it doesn't matter how much I sell if I can't get them to sell it; in other words, I've got to make sure it sells in their stores. Sometimes I have to say let's not send two items per store, let's just send one and then we will see how it does and then we will follow up with a replenishment. Most company vendors would never say something like that because they'd rather send all the merchandise the retailer is willing to take. But you don't want Wal-Mart's turns to be low, you don't want the buyer getting calls from the stores saying "What's this?," and you don't want that buyer to see mark-downs on your product; you want to make sure your product is successful for Wal-Mart. If you do that, they'll keep doing business with you and you'll be successful too.

In the typical supplier relationship only the retailer is truly focused on the retail customer. That's not the way it works at Wal-Mart, where vendors are also focused on selling their own products at retail. Sam Walton's approach to his vendors transformed the relationship between wholesalers, retailers, and customers.

RFID

Wal-Mart's commitment to technology has led to a strategy to equip every case of products in Wal-Mart's stores and distribution centers with RFID (radio frequency identification) tags. Many of the company's largest suppliers are already doing it. The current system allows a store manager to track sales of every product by day, by hour, by department, and by item. They use that information when they do merchandise planning and correction of errors for next year or next month. RFID will let them know where every piece of merchandise is in real time. Here's what a store manager said about the importance of this powerful new technology:

> Every afternoon Wal-Mart has teams which go out to every department in their stores and they scan all the products "outages" and low inventory products. That scanning may show there is none on the shelf but there are 12 pieces on hand in the stockroom. What if those 12 pieces aren't in their right bin in the stockroom? If that product is somewhere else, you've got to find it. That can be a tremendous hassle which may lead to lost sales. So they try to get that product on the shelves as quickly as they can so that they can get some sales off of it. If the scanning shows there is no product on the shelf and none in stockroom inventory, it will also tell you whether or not that item is coming in on tonight's truck. As soon as that product comes off the truck I want that case of product to go straight to the sales floor and onto the shelf. RFID is going to let you know exactly where it is at any given point in time. With RFID you can go find exactly where it is in the stockroom, the store, on a truck, or anywhere else in the supply chain. It is going to help with in stock and freight flow unbelievably, which will result in a 10 percent increase in sales across the board for Wal-Mart just by being able to stay in stock 100 percent of the time.

RFID is just one example of how Wal-Mart develops, commits, and uses innovative technology.

Pricing

Wal-Mart has shifted the consumer purchasing paradigm across the globe by offering the lowest possible prices on its products.

Sam Walton's everyday low-price strategy, coupled with offering products of all types and varieties, has turned Wal-Mart's Supercenters into destination stores for one-stop shoppers. Millions of shoppers venture into Wal-Mart's stores each week and if you stand at the door watching the customers as they exit, it seems like 99 percent of them have made a purchase. The reason for this is great prices. Here's how one of the store managers who worked with Sam Walton described his revolutionary pricing strategy:

> Everybody else was taking product from the manufacturer that had that little price tag stuck on it for "manufacturer's suggested retail price" and that is what everybody sold it for. Occasionally they would run big sales and mark it down. Mr. Sam bought that same merchandise and it might come into the store with a price tag of $15.00 and he said let it have that price tag of $15.00 but we're going to sell it every day for $12.97, which was unheard of in the industry. Everybody else had these tremendous margins up front and then they'd run sales or they'd run advertising to help drive business. You can hardly think of any large retailers today that sell merchandise for the manufacturer's suggested retail price; today, almost everybody discounts products at retail.

Sam Walton revolutionized retailing as we know it when he decided to do everything he could do to price his merchandise at the lowest possible level. When every other retailer was trying to get as much as they could for every product, he was trying to get as little as he could. He even worked with his suppliers to get them to figure out ways to make their operations more efficient so that they could sell him their products cheaper. Low prices attract customers to Wal-Mart's stores, and great service keeps them coming back for more.

Advertising

The senior vice president of stores at Wal-Mart once told me that the company doesn't need to put its products on sale because all of Wal-Mart's products are already on sale every day. That philosophy is Mr. Sam's everyday low-price (EDLP) strategy, which remains in place to this day. When Wal-Mart advertises, notice that their ads focus on public relations, community relations, recruiting, and EDLP but their ads don't talk about sales. Here's the way one of his store managers described the use of advertising:

> He didn't spend all that money on advertising to put his own name out there and his products out there. Even today you see a difference in advertising with Wal-Mart from a lot of others in that they are still advertising a brand and a concept rather than an item at a price. If you see a Home Depot ad they'll show you a grill and tell you how much you can get it for. Wal-Mart shows you a happy customer walking through the store or a "smiley face" slashing prices down the action alley. They continue to promote that low-price leader rather than advertising big sales to try to get you into the store. From the onset Mr. Sam revolutionized the industry, but what he really did was he built a sense of security in the shopping public. They continue to try to drive home what Wal-Mart stands for. Wal-Mart is always working to lower prices for you and that you can count on it to have a fair price every day. You can always depend on Wal-Mart to take care of you at the service desk, if for any reason you are unhappy. That's what really drives the company.

I get Wal-Mart's newspaper circulars periodically and in those circulars it focuses on EDLP while at the same time promoting its diverse workforce. Look at the photos of the people in their ads and you'll see men and women who actually work for the company, with their first names printed next to their pictures. Even their children get into the act of modeling clothes. Their advertising sends a message that the company is doing everything it can to keep prices at the lowest possible levels, *always*!

Merchandising

Mr. Sam used product merchandising as a way to teach merchant skills to his associates. He wanted his associates to understand the connection between displaying products well and increasing the velocity at which those products sold. He even encouraged them to select their own product and to display it creatively to see if they could sell more. Here's a great example of swimming upstream told to me by a store manager that illustrates how important product merchandising is to increasing sales:

> The discount store industry relies on apparel to improve the margins of the business overall. Every store you visited was flooding their sales floors with apparel. Wal-Mart took a different approach. We got a mandate at one of our year beginning meetings, we were all given a tape measure that measured exactly 36 inches and we were told to go back to our stores and take enough apparel off the floor even if we had to hang it up in the stock room in order to allow 36 inches of space between every single rack throughout the soft-lines area of the store. The theory was that we had allowed the apparel department to become so congested that shoppers couldn't even get into those areas with a shopping cart anymore. The directive we got was designed to open those areas back up. Wal-Mart did something that was taboo in retail by sending that merchandise back to the stockroom. While everyone else in retailing was packing their sales floor with apparel, we were removing it from our sales floor. When we opened up the sales floor we saw 20 percent increases in apparel sales.

The five self-professed keys to merchandising at Wal-Mart can be boiled down to stock it, price it right, show the value, take their money, and teach them.

Product Inventory

Many believe Wal-Mart's distribution capability is the single most important cost advantage it has over all other competitors. Some even talk about Wal-Mart as being more of a distribution or logistics-driven company as opposed to a merchandise-driven company. There is an old saying in retail that "out of stock is out of business." Wal-Mart does everything it can do to make certain products are on the shelves when customers shop its stores. Here's a story a Wal-Mart supplier told me about product distribution that captures Sam Walton's distribution advantage:

> Nothing is to stay in the warehouse for more than 24 hours; their warehouses are actually distribution centers. The product is delivered on one side of the building, which is a hundred and some odd number of acres big, and it is routed throughout the entire complex on miles and miles and miles of belts to a series of doors on the other side of the distribution center where the cases are loaded on trucks to go the stores. They call it cross-docking. The merchandise only spends a few hours in the distribution center. Other retailers pay interest on their inventory sitting in their warehouse. The longer it sits there, the more they're paying and those dollars come off their bottom line. Wal-Mart's philosophy is that nothing is going to sit here and grow roots in their distribution center. It can stop temporarily, "to catch its breath," but then it's got to move on, because within 24 hours they turn over everything in their distribution center.
>
> When we ship from our company we ship to their distribution centers and the cases are cross-docked and shipped out to their stores. We might send 8 to 10 pallets of merchandise at

a time by common carrier. From the time we ship it, to the time I can see on my computer the in stocks hitting the individual stores is usually within 3 to 8 days depending on how far away we are shipping. Our products sit in our own warehouse longer than it takes for them to flow it through Wal-Mart's distribution system.

As in this example, Mr. Sam was always challenging the conventional wisdom in retailing. By cross-docking, Sam Walton significantly lowered warehousing costs while simultaneously improving his ability to restock Wal-Mart's shelves.

New Store Concepts

Another great example of swimming upstream by Wal-Mart's executives is the creation of their new grocery store concept called "Neighborhood Market." These 40- to 50-thousand-square-foot stores are designed for the customer who prefers shopping for groceries in a smaller store. These stores also work well in urban areas where large real estate parcels are hard to find or nonexistent. Wal-Mart actually opens these stores in markets where it already has its Supercenters with little to no negative impact or cannibalization of their own sales. Neighborhood Markets have had a tremendous impact on the sales of existing grocery stores in those markets. Here's how a Wal-Mart Supercenter store manager describes this new store concept:

> A lot of people think it is crazy that Wal-Mart is opening Neighborhood Markets and they think it won't work. The reasoning behind it is that there are some people who on Friday evening or a Sunday morning don't want to fight the crowds at the Wal-Mart Supercenter to get a gallon of milk, a loaf of bread, and to pick up a prescription. To that point, when we opened the first Supercenter in Tallahassee, Florida, it did great

business but you know in that same town there were a couple of Publix, two or three Winn Dixie's, a couple of Albertson's, all still doing business. So there is a market out there for those grocery stores to still do business. The Neighborhood Market is designed to drop into markets where there are already existing Supercenters; and they aren't going to compete with the Supercenters they are going to compliment the Supercenters. They are a smaller format and they are easier to get in and out of and they are good-looking stores. They are designed to take market share from grocers like Winn Dixie and Publix. They aren't going to cannibalize business from the Supercenters like everyone is thinking; they are going to take away business from the grocery stores which are out there right now. They are even going to eat up business from people like CVS and Rite Aid which still do good business because everybody doesn't want to go into a Wal-Mart Supercenter and walk a country mile to get some shampoo and cold medicine and then go all the way over to the deli department. Some people just want to walk into a place quickly and leave. That's what the Neighborhood Market is allowing them to do.

Just as Sam Walton experimented with the Hypermarket concept, which led to the creation of the Supercenter, company leaders at Wal-Mart continue to experiment with new store concepts that complement their existing strengths.

Sam Walton, the innovator, was both a continuous learner and a change agent and he also wasn't afraid to imitate. He went out there and looked at other companies and tried to figure out one or two things his competitors were doing right. He wasn't concerned with what they were doing wrong. He'd take their good ideas back to Wal-Mart and try to improve upon them and even do them better. In the early days, though he was an innovator, he wasn't afraid to imitate the best practices of other retailers.

He was never happy with the status quo, and for this reason he actively led the charge to continuously improve every area of Wal-Mart's operation. Mr. Sam believed that acceptance of the status quo leads to complacency and in turn complacency zaps creativity. Today almost 2 million associates work for the company, and Mr. Sam would want all of their hearts and minds committed to improving every aspect of the business.

He used to take the position that if all of his competitors were approaching a business problem in an orthodox and traditional way, why don't we at Wal-Mart blaze our own trail in a completely new direction in an attempt to find a more efficient, cheaper, and faster way of accomplishing the same thing? The Wal-Mart way of doing business often conflicts with existing business paradigms about the way companies ought to conduct business. Because Wal-Mart is the largest company in the world, its successful challenges to existing business practices shift the paradigms for everyone. This forces Wal-Mart's competitors and its own suppliers to jump through hoops in an attempt to replicate Wal-Mart's trailblazing best practices.

Unfortunately for others, the Wal-Mart way, though often easy to understand, is painfully difficult for others to replicate. The reason for this is because most people and organizations don't have the cultural discipline to follow through. Wal-Mart, on the other hand, has a tradition of executing strategies and tactics with lockstep discipline. Its managers and associates embrace change and aren't afraid to try new ideas and new directions. In fact, innovation and change added to the excitement of working with Sam Walton.

In Wal-Mart's continuous search for operational excellence Wal-Mart leaders and its associates constantly challenge the status quo, try innovative solutions, and by doing so embrace change as a fond companion. For this reason, Wal-Mart adapts quickly to changes in the marketplace. If a strategy is working, they stick to it, constantly tweaking it to make it better and better. If something isn't working as well as they thought it should, they change it or do away with it outright and try something new. Company leaders aren't sentimental when it comes to making decisions and changing direction.

Everyone is encouraged and expected to recommend better ways to run the business, and there are no untouchable sacred cows anywhere in the company. As proof of that, I remember when an associate stood up at a Saturday morning meeting and challenged Sam Walton directly about the words to his most important cultural icon, the Wal-Mart cheer. At that time the cheer ended with the question, "Who is number 1?," to which everyone responded, "We are!" She challenged Mr. Sam's ending to the cheer by saying, "We're not number 1, the customer is number 1." She said that in her opinion the ending to the cheer should be, "Who is number 1? The customer." I remember watching Mr. Sam standing there on the stage and mulling that idea over in his mind. After contemplating the new idea, he asked everyone at the meeting what they thought of it. Immediately it was agreed to change the Wal-Mart cheer to reflect the new ending. To this day the cheer ends with "Who is number 1? The customer, *always*!"

One of Wal-Mart's store managers explained Sam Walton's concept of swimming upstream this way: "We always referred to it as, think outside of the box or sometimes we'd say stop and think like a customer. Unless you could get out of the mentality of just running the business every day you'd get stuck in the trenches executing." Mr. Sam wanted everybody to always question everything we were doing and to look for a better way to do it. That meant going in the opposite direction, sometimes trying some things that others weren't willing to try. Mr. Sam would be the first to tell you that when you swim upstream you will make mistakes but every once in a while, you'll find a breakthrough idea and that one idea can make all of those previous mistakes worthwhile.

Our People Make the Difference

If you really break down Mr. Sam's 10 rules for success you'll find one is about customer service, one is about managing expenses, one is about personal commitment, one is about risk taking, and six are about how to treat people!

Have you ever wondered why Wal-Mart located its headquarters in the middle of the Ozark Mountains? You might surmise it was all part of Sam Walton's grand design plan for the future of Wal-Mart for purposes of product distribution. Logistically, this theory seems to make sense since Bentonville is pretty darn close to the geographic center of the United States. But that's not the logistical reason Sam Walton located there. You see, there is an area near Bentonville called "Four Corners," where Kansas, Oklahoma, Missouri, and Arkansas converge. Locating his first Ben Franklin Store in this area allowed him to pursue his second passion in life, bird hunting. His forward-thinking logical mind figured out he could get four different state bird hunting licenses by living there, allowing him to load his bird dogs up in the back of his old pickup truck and drive a short distance to hunt quail and pheasant all year round.

Just imagine how that decision, to locate the company's headquarters in the Ozarks, impacted Sam Walton's ability to find and hire great people to help him achieve his retail dreams. By necessity, as his company grew, Mr. Sam was forced to hire his company leaders and associates from the local labor pool around northwest Arkansas, which was composed of mostly farmers, teachers, government workers, and rural business people from southeast Kansas, northeast Oklahoma, southern Missouri, and northwest Arkansas. Though fortunate the local work ethic was strong in the area, he was forced to hire a completely naïve and inexperienced retail workforce—well-intentioned people with no prerequisite corporate experience. Out of necessity, Mr. Sam discovered a new wave hiring strategy out in rural America called "hire for attitude, and train for results."

When I went to Wal-Mart's home office, I was shocked and awed by the decision-making process used to fill open job positions. For me, the staffing paradigm shifted once I had a chance to view Wal-Mart's diametrically opposed view of what it took to be successful in a *Fortune* 500 company. As far as I'm concerned, Sam Walton reinvented and redefined the standards for world-class staffing by focusing on hiring inexperienced, enthusiastic people with fire in their belly. He hired can-do people with an optimistic outlook and positive attitude, trained them in the Wal-Mart way, and then set extremely aggressive standards for individual and team performance. Substance is by far more important than form at the world's largest and most successful company.

The kinds of people Sam Walton hired were ordinary folks, many of whom were previously farmers. Mr. Sam wasn't afraid to hire ordinary people with good attitudes and a strong work ethic. Promotion from within was the standard that Sam Walton termed "picking 'em green." Amazingly, most of those promoted from within were very successful in their new jobs. What those promoted lacked in experience they made up for through dedication and hard work. As a result of "picking 'em green"some failures were inevitable, ending in a small number of demotions. Mr. Sam Walton referred to demotions as "steppin' down" from a higher level of responsibility job to a lower responsibility job. Unlike the stigma attached to demotions at other companies, being promoted and then demoted was not a badge of dishonor at Wal-Mart. "Steppin, down" was just attributed to being inexperienced as a result of having been "picked green."

Wal-Mart is one of the few big companies in America where it's still possible for an individual to join the company without bringing prior knowledge and experience and still have the chance to achieve their personal career dreams. There are examples of this success story played out throughout the company—non-degreed individuals hired off the farm with no experience who have worked hard and assumed highly responsible positions. Promoting inexperienced people is actually a blessing in disguise as it allows the company to train its leaders in the Wal-Mart way of doing things.

The ability to take a group of people with little prior experience in business and shape them into a high-performing team is one of Sam Walton's greatest achievements. The following quote from Sam Walton captures his belief that "our people make the difference:"

> I'd like to say that we're a diverse collection of mostly average people—almost a melting pot, if you will, of former retailers, housewives, college trainees, and just people from all walks of life. But the factor that has set us apart from the beginning are those qualities hidden inside for the most part in our associates that have seemed to confound the experts. One of those qualities I'm contending our people have is a strong will to win. Our people want to win so badly that they just go out there and do it. Even though everybody has told them they can't succeed, they just go out there and succeed anyway! They have to know instinctively that determination and perseverance are far more important than many of the technical and theoretical approaches often advocated by the "experts." Our folks don't expect something for nothing, and they don't expect things to come easily. Our method of success, as I see it, is ACTION with a capital "A," and a lot of hard work mixed in.
>
> We've said it through the years—Do It, Try It, Fix It. Not a bad approach and it works. There are a lot of people out there who have great ideas, but nothing in the world is cheaper than a good idea without any action behind it. The problem usually is finding someone who is willing to implement it. We must continue to urge our associates to be implementers—action-oriented doers. It's a whole lot more fun

and it accomplishes so much more. Being action oriented is so important, and thank goodness our Wal-Mart team and associates have been, and are geared to be action oriented. Let's not lose it.

In Wal-Mart we must treat our people with real genuine respect and courtesy. Your people aren't numbers on your own success chart. They're real people and deserve to be treated that way. We've got to get to know our people—their families, their problems, their hopes, and their ambitions—if we are to help them grow and develop. We must appreciate and praise them as individuals. Show your concern daily.

Leaders always put their people before themselves. I really like this one. If you forget all else that's been written here, remember the following, if you want a successful business, your people must feel that you are working for them—not that they are working for you. And it really should be that way. As a leader, your most important job is helping your people become the best they can be and reach the absolute peak of their potential. If you're able to do that, your business will take care of itself. No one can fail with a group of independent, motivated, excited, and happy people working hard to reach their own individual goals.*

From this quote you can sense the sincerity of Sam Walton and the fact that he truly cared about the associates at Wal-Mart. He believed it was his associates that were responsible for the incredible success of the company. Interestingly enough, you'll find if you take a close look at Mr. Sam's 10 rules, 6 of the 10 rules have something to do with the way he believed you should treat people. Here's the list of 10 Rules; Rules 2 through 7 that are "bolded" and represent Sam Walton's 6 rules related specifically

---

*Quote from Sam Walton excerpted from *Wal-Mart World* (Wal-Mart's company magazine).

to how leaders need to treat the people who work for their organization:

Rule #1 COMMIT to achieving success and always be passionate.

Rule #2 SHARE SUCCESS with those who have helped you.

Rule #3 MOTIVATE yourself and others to achieve your dreams.

Rule #4 COMMUNICATE with people and show you care.

Rule #5 APPRECIATE and recognize people for their efforts and results.

Rule #6 CELEBRATE your own and other's accomplishments.

Rule #7 LISTEN to others and learn from their ideas.

Rule #8 EXCEED EXPECTATIONS of customers and others.

Rule #9 CONTROL EXPENSES and save your way to prosperity.

Rule #10 SWIM UPSTREAM, be different, and challenge the status quo.

If you take Sam Walton's 10 rules and distill them down, you'll see that six of his rules deal specifically with how he believed you should treat people, one is about your personal commitment, one is about taking care of your customers, one is about controlling costs, and one is about taking risks. With this in mind, I can simplify his list of 10 rules into the following five "buckets":

1. Communicate a clear business strategy and tactics
2. Take care of your employees
3. Control your costs
4. Exceed your customer's expectations
5. Challenge the status quo by taking calculated risks

Let me share with you some final thoughts about each of these high-impact areas.

Communicate a Clear Business Strategy and Tactics

Every week of the year Wal-Mart leaders conduct one of their famous Saturday morning leadership meetings at the Bentonville, Arkansas, headquarters. As many as 500 managers representing all functional areas of the company's headquarters are in attendance. Wal-Mart's executives discuss the company's current performance and more importantly focus the leadership team on the goals for the weeks to come. By meeting every week of the year with leaders from every department, the top executives are able to focus everyone on the same set of goals. Functional department agendas, or what I've heard termed "functional silos" don't exist. Everyone is focused on the overall corporate retail agenda of the company. If I were to boil down a recommendation for you to create a singularity of focus, it would be communicate, communicate, communicate! Communication of strategy using one voice is one of the great success secrets of Sam Walton. The other half of the success equation is follow up, follow up, and follow up every week of the year to ensure the tactical execution is actually happening!

Take Care of Your Employees

Mr. Sam required the executives and managers from Wal-Mart's headquarters to travel out to the stores every week of the year. He called it MBWA, or management by wandering around! He required them to meet with the associates of the company and to meet with customers. During these meetings the real issues were brought to their attention by their own employees and their customers, allowing them to respond quickly with solutions. Mr. Sam Walton called the employees at Wal-Mart "associates" (business partners), the managers he referred to as "coaches," and his customers were "friends or neighbors." Sam Walton expected company leaders to take the time to get to know the associates by name, and in the process, the associates would in turn care about the goals of the company. Sam Walton used to say, "If you take care of your people, your people will take care of the customer and the business will take care of itself."

Control Your Costs

I learned an acronym from Wal-Mart's Sam's Club division: HEATKTE (a pseudo–American-Indian word) stands for, *High Expectations Are The Key To Everything.* Empowered associates are held accountable for managing and cutting costs wherever they possibly can. Culturally Mr. Sam called this value, "ownership" and the associates acting as true business partners utilized company resources as if they were paying for them out of their own pockets! Managing expenses efficiently is one of Wal-Mart's towering strengths and drops billions of dollars to its bottom line. By establishing management and associate standards for controlling wasteful practices, communicating those expectations to everyone, and holding managers and associates accountable, company leaders have turned cost control into a competitive advantage.

Exceed Your Customer's Expectations

Mr. Sam directed Wal-Mart's leaders to have one agenda: satisfying customers. Everything else they do is secondary to their primary goal of enhancing, improving, or delivering knock-your- socks-off service to customers in their stores. Regardless of what department an associate works in or what job he or she does for the company, everyone at Wal-Mart is required to think like a retail merchant. It makes no difference whether an associate works in accounting, human resources, distribution, fleet, real estate, advertising, buying, or technology; everyone is focused on serving or improving service to the customer. Mr. Sam even had a 10-foot rule that states that if a customer comes within 10 feet of an associate, that associate must drop everything and approach the customer and offer assistance.

Challenge the Status Quo by Taking Calculated Risks

Whoever said, "If it ain't broke, don't fix it" never met Sam Walton. Mr. Sam was a continuous learner and a risk taker who was constantly tinkering with the status quo. He embraced a Japanese quality concept called *kaizen*, which roughly translated means "to take something apart and put it back together again in a better way." Mr. Sam's idea behind *kaizen* was to get everyone at Wal-Mart to constantly pursue small improvements to operational processes that over time would lead to big improvements. Associates are even taught to flow-chart processes and are then given the authority to implement changes that reduce costs or save time, energy, and effort. Change is a way of life at Wal-Mart, and Sam Walton embraced change as a welcome friend!

Sam Walton's 10 rules for success are applicable in other retail companies, but more importantly they are applicable in other industries. I truly believe his 10 rules will help improve the operations of retailers, nonretailers, manufacturers, and suppliers as well as the operations of local, state, and federal government, churches, hospitals, and educational institutions. Of course, companies small and large will benefit from the knowledge gained from the world's most successful company. By learning, embracing, and implementing the leadership lessons of Sam Walton and Wal-Mart, you'll be well on your way to improving your own chances of success. Wal-Mart has forever changed the world of business competition. Adapting, changing, and innovating are critical success components for those who want to compete, survive, and thrive in the highly competitive Wal-Mart world created by Sam Walton!

The Ten Rules of Sam Walton is a glimpse into Sam Walton's coaching playbook and by using his tested methods, you can transform your organization. For this reason, you should use the 10 rules of Mr. Sam as a blueprint for your success. Who better to learn from than the founder of the largest, most innovative, and most successful company in the history of the world?

About the Author

Michael Bergdahl is a full-time motivational speaker, author, consultant, and writer. Bergdahl worked in Bentonville, Arkansas, for Wal-Mart, as the Director of People for the headquarters office, where he worked directly with Sam Walton. It was Sam Walton who gave Bergdahl the nickname "Bird Dawg"! Previous to Wal-Mart he worked for PepsiCo's Frito-Lay Division in the sales organization and in headquarters staff assignments. He has recent experience as a turnaround specialist who participated in two successful business turnarounds at American Eagle Outfitters and Waste Management.

Bergdahl has appeared on CNN, CNBC, CNN FN, CBS National Radio, and Bloomberg TV. He is considered an authority on Wal-Mart. His articles have appeared in *Retail Merchandiser*, *Investor's Business Daily*, *Convenience Store News*, *Progressive Grocer*, *Convenience Store Decisions Magazine*, the Grocery Manufacturer Association's *Forum Magazine*, the National Community Pharmacists Association's *America's Pharmacist Magazine*, the American Management Association's *MWorld Magazine*, and the *NACS Magazine*.

He has written a book about his experiences working for the world's largest retailer entitled: *What I Learned from Sam Walton: How to Compete and Thrive in a Wal-Mart World*, which was published in the United States and internationally by John Wiley in August 2004.

Bergdahl is a motivational speaker, who is one part business, one part inspiration, one part storyteller, and one part entertainer. He has spoken at association and business conferences, domestically and internationally, to groups that are interested in learning about the success secrets of Wal-Mart and Sam Walton. On his web site, *www.michaelbergdahl.net*, is a link to his "Wal-Mart Competition" blog.

Index

◄●►